EASY KETO FOR BUSY PEOPLE

The Step by Step Cookbook Guide with over 110+ Quick Delicious, Friendly and Easy Recipes for Health and Weight Loss with Ketogenic Diet

MARK WILLIAM

Copyright © 2019 Mark William

All rights reserved.

All rights reserved. No part of this guide may be reproduced in any form without permission in writing from the publisher except in the case of brief quotations embodied in critical articles or reviews.

Legal & Disclaimer

The information contained in this book and its contents is not designed to replace or take the place of any form of medical or professional advice; and is not meant to replace the need for independent medical, financial, legal or other professional advice or services, as may be required. The content and information in this book have been provided for educational and entertainment purposes only.

The content and information contained in this book have been compiled from sources deemed reliable, and it is accurate to the best of the Author's knowledge, information, and belief. However, the Author cannot guarantee its accuracy and validity and cannot be held liable for any errors and/or omissions. Further, changes are periodically made to this book as and when needed. Where appropriate and/or necessary, you must consult a professional (including but not limited to your doctor, attorney, financial advisor or such other professional advisor) before using any of the suggested remedies, techniques or information in this book.

Upon using the contents and information contained in this book, you agree to hold harmless the Author from and against any damages, costs, and expenses, including any legal fees potentially resulting from the application of any of the information provided by this book. This disclaimer applies to any loss, damages or injury caused by the use and application whether directly or indirectly, of any advice or information presented, whether for breach of contract, tort, negligence, personal injury, criminal intent, or under any other cause of action.

You agree to accept all risks of using the information presented inside this book.

You agree that by continuing to read this book, where appropriate and/or necessary, you shall consult a professional (including but not limited to your doctor, attorney, or financial advisor or such other advisor as needed) before using any of the suggested remedies, techniques, or information in this book.

Table of Contents

Table of Contents 1
Introduction 7
What is Keto Diet? 8
Foods to Eat and Avoid 9
Day-to-Day Benefits of Keto Diet 12
Are there any side effects, risks or dangers with KETO? 12
Key to Success 13
1. BREAKFAST 15
Sausage Breakfast Sandwich 15
Cinnamon Roll Knots 16
Sausage and Egg Breakfast Bowl 18
No-Egg Breakfast Bake with Sausage and Peppers 19
Meat Bagel 21
Fluffy Blueberry Pancakes 23
Steak and Eggs 24
Creamy Kale and Eggs 25
Freezer Breakfast Pockets 26
McMuffin Sausage and Egg Breakfast Sandwich 27
Broccoli Cheese Breakfast Casserole 29
Black Forest Mocha Chia Seed Pudding 30
2. SNACKS AND DRINKS 32
Mini Taco Egg Muffins 32
Cheesy Garlic Bread Muffins 33
Buffalo Chicken Sausage Balls 35

Corn Dog Nuggets 36

Mini Pizza Muffins 38

Rosemary Parmesan Crackers 39

Mini Pepper Nachos 41

Bloody Mary 43

Homemade Coffee Liqueur 44

Minty Moscow Mule 45

Boozy Root beer Float 47

3. SOUPS AND SALADS 51

Roasted Tomato & Garlic Soup 48

Easy Low Carb Chicken Soup 49

Poblano Chicken Soup 50

Hearty Ham and Green Bean Soup 52

Creamy Pumpkin & Sausage Chowder 53

Tomato Basil Soup 55

Southwestern Pumpkin Cheddar Soup 56

BLT Lobster Roll Salad 58

Grilled Chicken & Baby Bok Choy Salad 60

Creamy Shrimp & Cauliflower Salad 62

Caprese Zucchini Noodle Pasta Salad 63

4. DESSERT 65

Caramel Cake 65

Classic New York Keto Cheesecake 67

Cinnamon Roll Coffee Cake 68

Chocolate Walnut Torte 70

Kentucky Butter Cake 72

Pecan Pie Cheesecake 74

Gingerbread Cake Roll 77

Pumpkin Pie Cupcakes 79

Peanut Butter Blossoms 80

Oatmeal Chocolate Chip Cookies 82

Chocolate Hazelnut Sandwich Cookies 84

Cranberry Pecan Biscotti 86

5. SEASONING 88

Blackened Seasoning 88

Jamaican Jerk Seasoning 89

Gingerbread Spice Mix 91

Montreal Steak Seasoning 91

BBQ Seasoning 92

Lemon Pepper Seasoning 93

Pumpkin Pie Spice 94

Taco Seasoning 95

Dry Ranch Seasoning 96

Poultry Seasoning 97

6. MEAT 99

Cabbage Beef Skillet 99

Beef Stroganoff Meatballs 100

Crockpot Beef Stew 102

Unstuffed Cabbage Soup 103

Beef Taquitos 105

Italian Meatball Casserole 106

Mongolian Beef 108

Italian Pork & Parmesan Meatballs 109

Pork Egg Roll In A Bowl 112

Bacon Covered Meatloaf 113

Ground Pork Tacos 114

Spinach And Italian Sausage Stuffed Pork Tenderloin 115

Apple Dijon Pork Chops 117

7. FISH 119

Salmon With Creamy Dill Sauce 119

Salmon With Bacon & Tomato Cream Sauce 120

Avocado & Basil Salmon 122

Salmon & Asparagus Foil Packs 124

Salmon With Tzatziki Sauce 125

Salmon Stuffed Avocado 127

Salmon Ceviche 128

Roasted Salmon With Parmesan Dill Crust 129

Lemon Butter Baked Cod 130

Parmesan Crusted Cod 132

Buttered Cod Skillet 133

Shrimp & Bacon Zoodle Alfredo 135

8. CHICKEN 136

Chicken Cacciatore 136

One-Pot Bacon Garlic Chicken and Spinach Dinner 137

Lemon and Herb Roast Chicken 138

Chicken with 40 Garlic Cloves 140

Creamy Sun Dried Tomato and Parmesan Chicken Zoodles 141

Sheet Pan Chicken Fajitas 143

Italian Chicken Meal Prep 144

Chicken, Avocado and Goat Cheese Salad 146

Creamy Pesto Parmesan Chicken 148

One Pan Pizza Chicken 149

Chicken with Poblano Peppers and Cream 150

Caprese Hasselback Chicken 152

Shredded Chicken Chili 153

9. SMOOTHIES 155

Acai Almond Butter Smoothie 155

Blueberry Galaxy Smoothie 156

Clean and Green Smoothie 157

Frozen Berry Shake 158

Green Low-Carb Breakfast Smoothie 159

Minty Green Protein Smoothie 160

Blueberry Coconut Chia Smoothie 161

Cinnamon Almond Butter Breakfast Shake 162

Chocolate Coconut Keto Smoothie Bowl 163

Chocolate Mint Avocado Smoothie 164

Keto Green Smoothie 165

Cucumber Green Tea Detox Smoothie 166

No-Sugar Kale & Coconut Shake 167

Chai Pumpkin Keto Smoothie 168

Raspberry Avocado Smoothie 169
Conclusion 170

Introduction

I want to thank you and congratulate you for buying this book..

This book contains proven steps and strategies on how to get to know more about the Ketogenic Diet and how it teaches the body to convert stubborn and stored fats into usable energy thereby speeding up the weight loss process.

One of the main reasons why the Ketogenic Diet is popular is because this is the only dietary program that aids in melting the visceral fat or those fats that are stored around the abdominal cavity and other internal organs of the body. Ask long-term dieters and those who are into body sculpting and they would tell you that the visceral fat are the hardest and the last to overcome in their pursuit of lean and well-sculpt figures.

For those who are new to the Ketogenic diet, it should be noted that this is considered to be a highly restrictive diet. The body's production of glucose is gradually lowered to a minimum when on this diet. What this means to say is that starchy vegetables, grains, and even some fruits that are high in sugar are not advised to be included in your diet. Instead, you must consume good fats, meat, nuts, seeds, and dairy products.

Say goodbye to carbs and hello to more fulfilling meals with the recipes that you can make pretty quick and take to your work! Just look through the recipe list and get ready

to make cream cheese pancakes for breakfast, a zesty roasted lemon chicken for dinner, zucchini parmesan chips and so much more!

What is Keto Diet?

The ketogenic diet is a low carbohydrate, high-fat diet. Maintaining this diet is an excellent tool for weight loss. More importantly, according to an increasing number of studies, it reduces risk factors for diabetes, heart diseases, stroke, Alzheimer's, epilepsy, and more1-6. On the keto diet, your body will enter a metabolic state called ketosis.

While in ketosis, your body is using ketone bodies for energy instead of glucose. Ketone bodies are derived from fat and are a much more stable, steady source of energy than glucose, which has derived from carbohydrates. Entering ketosis usually takes anywhere from 3 days to a week. Once you're in ketosis, you'll be using fat for energy, instead of carbs. It includes the fat you eat and stored body fat.

The Ketogenic diet was primarily created as a way to control the effects of epilepsy in children. This was based on the principle of ketosis, which reduces the frequency, duration, and intensity of seizures naturally through burning unyielding fats. However, recently, this diet became popular among dieters when it was proven to be effective in weight loss.

The Ketosis State

The body goes through the state of ketosis the moment the glucose from carbohydrates are strictly minimized from one's daily diet. Glucose is said to be the main fuel of the brain, but there are times when the brain pushes the pancreas to produce significant amounts of ketone bodies. These ketones are water soluble molecules that absorb fats in the adipose tissues. These are the ones that the brain absorbs and the body used as energy source. Ketosis happens after 2 to 7 days of slow but steady glucose or calorie removal. It is during these times when the brain is already burning lipids at a rapid pace. Ketosis should be maintained until your desired weight is achieved. Remember that this should be done consistently that any cheat day could only lead you back to square 1.

Things to Remember

A healthy diet is not solution to anything in and of itself; it must be applied as part of a healthy lifestyle in order to see maximum results. Think of the ketogenic diet as the foundation of your new body. If you want to build something truly special on top of it then design your lifestyle with that goal in mind. Cutting out junk food goes without saying, as does ditching bad habits such as smoking and drinking. Exercise, too, will take you to heights you never thought was possible. So, as you explore these delectable dishes and embark on the keto diet, try not to neglect other areas or responsibility.

Let this be the start of something great!

Foods to Eat and Avoid
To reach the state of ketosis, you must eat between 25 and 50 grams of carbohydrates per day maximum (about 5 to 10% of your energy), that is to say the equivalent of a banana or a yogurt in individual format... for 24 hours. In comparison, someone who eats "normally" gets about 50% of his energy from carbohydrates (so between 250g and 300g of carbohydrates).

Interestingly, a single fatty meal does not lead you to ketosis. To reach this state, your body must be short of carbs at least 3 to 4 days. Then, if you stay the course for 3 to 4 weeks (period of keto-adaptation), the proportion of energy that your brain will seek through the ketone bodies will increase increase gradually, until reaching about 70%. There you will be in real ketosis.

A small portion of the energy your brain uses will continue to come from carbohydrates that will be produced specifically for it from the fat in your body (if that's not a favored treatment!).

So concretely, you have to eat foods low in carbohydrates and high in fat. For example:

Foods to Eat

- Red meat
- Bacon
- Ham

- Sausage
- Fat fish (salmon, trout, sardines, mackerel, tuna ...)
- Butter
- Cheese
- Nuts and seeds
- Cream 35%
- Mayonnaise
- Low-Carb Vegetables
- Meat and Poultry
- Eggs
- Coconut Oil
- Berries
- Avocados.
- Shirataki Noodles
- Olives
- Unsweetened Coffee and Tea
- Dark Chocolate and Cocoa Powder
- Plain Greek Yogurt and Cottage Cheese.
- Olive Oil
- Etc.

The foods you should not eat are:

- Potatoes (including french fries!)
- Rice pasta
- Bread
- All grains
- Artificial sweeteners
- Refined fats / oils
- "Low-fat", "low-carb" and "zero-carb" products
- Factory-farmed pork and fish
- Processed foods containing carrageenan

- Milk
- Tropical fruit (pineapple, mango, banana, papaya, etc.)
- Mainly for health reasons, avoid soy products
- Alcoholic, sweet drinks (beer, sweet wine, cocktails, etc.)
- Legumes Etc.

If you inadvertently eat too much carbohydrate and you quit ketosis, your body will need at least 3 days to 1 month to return to KETO - mode. The state of ketosis is defined by a specific concentration (0.5 mM and more) of ketone bodies in your blood. Ketones are molecules that are produced when your glucose reserves become too low to support your brain.

When that happens, your brain (which likes sugar a lot, but is able to compromise, a good guy you know) is forced to fuel with what remains: fat. But the fat is not able to get to the brain as it is, so they are broken down into acetyl-CoA, and then converted by your liver into ketone bodies to feed your friend's brain.

To confirm that your body is in ketosis, there are tabs on which you can urinate and tell you if you are. Another device similar to the breathalyzer can analyze your degree of ketosis from an expiration.

Why We Use Keto Diet for Weight Loss

Studies consistently show that those who eat a low carb, high fat diet rather than a high carb, low-fat diet:

- Lose more weight and body fat
- Have better levels of good cholesterol
- Have reduced blood sugar and insulin resistance
- Experience a decrease in appetite
- Have reduced triglyceride levels (fat molecules in the blood that causes heart disease)
- Have significant reductions in blood pressure, leading to a reduction of heart disease and stroke.

Day-to-Day Benefits of Keto Diet

The keto diet doesn't only provide long-term benefits! When you're on keto, you can expect to:

- Lose body fat.
- Have consistent energy levels during the day
- Stay satiated after meals longer, with less snacking and overeating
- Longer satiation and constant energy levels are due to the majority of calories coming from fat, which is slower to digest and calorically denser.
- Eating low carb also eliminates blood glucose spikes and crashes. You won't have sudden blood sugar drops leaving you feeling weak and disoriented.
- The keto diet's primary goal is to keep you in nutritional ketosis all the time. If you're just getting started with your keto diet, you should eat up to 25 grams of carbs per day.
- Once you're in ketosis for long enough, you become keto-adapted, or fat adapted.
- It is when your glycogen decreases; you carry less water weight; muscle endurance increases and you are overall energy levels are higher.
- Another benefit of being keto-adapted is that you can eat 50 grams of net carbs a day to maintain ketosis.

Are there any side effects, risks or dangers with KETO?

The side effects are undeniable, but they are mostly present during the first 3 to 4 weeks of keto-adaptation.

Breath

One of the most glaring side effects is that your breath feels fruity because of acetone, a volatile ketone that is released through your airways. To give you an idea of the smell, acetone is also the product used in nail polish remover, so your breath has the air of "remover"!

Constipation

With such a radical change, the bacteria in your intestinal flora are a little shocked. As they adjust to handle as much fat, you have a good chance of being constipated. If it persists after several

weeks, it's a good sign that you do not eat enough fiber. To fix that, drink more water, move more and eat foods high in fiber, but low in carbohydrates to keep you out of your ketosis (eg nuts, seeds, broccoli, cauliflower, spinach, etc. .

Keto "flu"

Influenza-like symptoms may occur at the beginning of the keto-adaptation (eg, dizziness, fatigue, insomnia, sugar cravings, slow-motion brain, etc.). Normally, it fades after the first few weeks.

Key to Success

The ketogenic diet works on the basis of using fat metabolism to provide energy to the body rather than using carbohydrate or sugar metabolism. These ketones that are produced after fat metabolism are used to fuel energy to the body.

There the key to being successful on the keto diet and the main source of calories in your everyday diet. In total, there are three macros that you need to watch carefully - fats, protein, and carbs.

Since the keto diet is high in fat, that's where you'll get a majority of your daily calories. To keep things in check, the general ratio of macros you need on the keto diet is 70% fat, 25% protein, and 5% carbohydrates.

When you finally kick start your keto diet, your daily intake of net carbs shouldn't exceed no more than 20g. No excuses. Even if you calculate beforehand and you're recommended daily macro carb count is 27g for example, you still need to stay at below 20g when you start out.

Starting any new diet can be tough, especially when your diet is limited to only certain types of foods. Eating the same dozen food items can quickly become boring, which may make the "off-limit" foods even more tempting. This cookbook offers a compilation of recipes that will allow your diet to remain varied while sticking to the ketogenic diet itself.

This cookbook also offers a range of recipes that require a little more time an can be to cooked by anyone especially those mornings when you are in a hurry for your office. This Keto Diet Cookbook offers 110+ different recipes that will help you stick to this diet to achieve your various health goals.

1. BREAKFAST

Sausage Breakfast Sandwich

Serves: 1

Cook Time: 5 minutes

Ingredients

- 2 sausage patties
- 1 egg
- 1 tbsp cream cheese
- 2 tbsp sharp cheddar
- 1/4 medium avocado, sliced
- 1/4–1/2 tsp sriracha (to taste)
- Salt, pepper to taste

Directions

1. In skillet over medium heat, cook sausages per package instructions and set aside
2. In small bowl place cream cheese and sharp cheddar. Microwave for 20-30 seconds until melted
3. Mix cheese with sriracha, set aside
4. Mix egg with seasoning and make small omelette
5. Fill omelette with cheese sriracha mixture and assemble sandwich

Nutritional Facts:

- Calories: 603

- Fats: 54g
- Carbohydrates: 4g
- Proteins: 22g

Cinnamon Roll Knots

Serves: 10

Cook Time: 10 minutes

Ingredients

- FOR THE KETO DOUGH:
- 96 g almond flour
- 24 g coconut flour
- 2 teaspoons xanthan gum
- 2 teaspoons baking powder
- 1/4 teaspoon kosher salt
- 2 teaspoons apple cider vinegar
- 1 egg lightly beaten
- 5 teaspoons water as needed
- FOR THE KETO CINNAMON ROLL KNOTS FILLING
- 14 g grass-fed butter or coconut butter/oil, melted
- 3-4 tablespoons golden erythritol or xylitol, to taste
- 1-2 teaspoons cinnamon to taste
- FOR THE CREAM CHEESE GLAZE (OPTIONAL, BUT HIGHLY SUGGESTED!)
- 30 g cream cheese softened
- 14 g grass-fed butter softened
- 1-2 tablespoons powdered erythritol
- 1/2 teaspoon vanilla extract
- pinch kosher salt

- 1-3 teaspoons almond milk as needed (optional)
-

Directions

1. Preheat oven to 350°F/180°C. Line a baking tray with a baking mat or parchment paper.
2. FOR THE KETO DOUGH:
3. Add almond flour, coconut flour, xanthan gum, baking powder and salt to food processor. Pulse until thoroughly combined.
4. Pour in apple cider vinegar with the food processor running. Once it has distributed evenly, pour in the egg. Followed by the water. Stop the food processor once the dough forms into a ball. The dough will be sticky to touch.
5. Wrap dough in cling film and knead it through the plastic for a minute or two. Think of it a bit like a stress ball. Allow dough to rest for 10 minutes (and up to 5 days in the fridge).
6. FOR THE KETO CINNAMON ROLL KNOTS
7. Roll out the rested dough between two sheets of parchment paper with a rolling pin until roughly 10x10 inches in size. To get a perfect square, simply trim the uneven edges, patch them up and keep rolling until evenly sized.
8. Assemble by brushing with melted butter and sprinkling with the cinnamon 'sugar' (to taste- we do 3TBS sweetener with 1 1/2 teaspoons cinnamon). Fold the dough in half and cut into 8-10 strips with a pastry cutter. Twist and roughly make into knots, pinching the dough together to seal closed (it'll naturally form into rounds as you twist). You can freeze the cinnamon roll knots at this point for a month or two, and bake straight from the freezer (adding a few more minutes in the oven).
9. Place the knots in prepared tray and bake for 8-12 minutes (we do 10), until they just begin to brown. You want to only bake them briefly so they stay moist and doughy, otherwise you'll get cookies (still good, but not ideal!).

10. While your cinnamon knots are in the oven. Cream together with an electric mixer the cream cheese and butter until light and fluffy. Beat in the powdered sweetener, vanilla extract and salt. If you want it more of a drizzling consistency, add a few teaspoons of almond milk to thin it out.
11. These guys are best served warm straight from the oven, with a generous drizzle of cream cheese glaze. But they also do re-warm quite well.

Nutritional Facts:

- Calories: 102
- Fats: 8g
- Carbohydrates: 3g
- Proteins: 3g

Sausage and Egg Breakfast Bowl

Serves: 1

Cook Time: 25 minutes

Ingredients

- 200 grams radishes
- 3.5 oz ground sausage (we used Bob Evans Savory Sage ground sausage)
- 1/4 cup Shredded Cheddar Cheese
- 1 large Egg
- 1/4 tsp Pink Himalayan Salt
- 1/4 tsp black pepper

Directions

1. Cook sausage in a medium high heat until fully cooked through. Remove sausage from pan and set aside leaving grease in the pan.
2. Cup up radishes into bite sized pieces and add to the pan. Season with salt and pepper.
3. Cook until radishes become tender to bite or easily pierced with a fork. It should take 8-12 minutes.
4. In the meantime fry up an egg to your preference and set aside. We like ours over easy so the yolk can spill into all the layers!
5. Once radishes are fully cooked layer with sausage, cheese and egg. The warm layers should melt the cheese.
6. Serve warm and enjoy!

Nutritional Facts:

- Calories: 617
- Fats: 50g
- Carbohydrates: 7g
- Proteins: 32g

No-Egg Breakfast Bake with Sausage and Peppers

Serves: 4

Cook Time: 35 minutes

Ingredients

- 1 large green bell pepper, chopped
- 1 large red bell pepper, chopped (or use any color of peppers you prefer)
- 1 tsp. + 1/2 tsp. olive oil

- Spike Seasoning to taste (or use any all-purpose seasoning mix that you like the flavor of)
- fresh-ground black pepper to taste
- 12 links (about 10 oz.) turkey or pork breakfast sausage links (I used Low-Fat and Pre-Cooked Jimmy Dean Turkey Breakfast Sausage, for low-carb or Keto diet you should use pork sausage or other higher-fat sausage of your choice)
- 1/2 cup Mozzarella, grated

Directions

1. Preheat oven to 450F/230C.
2. Spray a medium-sized baking dish with non-stick spray.
3. Cut away the stem part and cut out seeds of the red and green bell pepper and chop peppers into pieces about an inch across.
4. Put peppers into the baking dish, toss with 1 teaspoon olive oil, sprinkle with Spike Seasoning and fresh-ground black pepper, and put the dish in the oven and bake 20 minutes.
5. While the peppers cook, heat the rest of the olive oil in a non-stick pan, add the sausages and cook over medium-high heat until they're nicely browned on all sides, about 10-12 minutes.
6. Remove to cutting board, line them up, and cut sausages into thirds.
7. When the peppers have cooked for 20 minutes, stir in the sausages and bake 5 minutes more.
8. Remove from oven, turn oven to BROIL, sprinkle the grated Mozzarella over the sausage-pepper combination and put back in oven and broil 1-2 minutes, or until the cheese is nicely melted and starting to brown.
9. Serve hot.
10. DIRECTIONS FOR ALTERNATIVE, SLIGHTLY EASIER BUT LONGER METHOD:
11. Preheat oven to 400F/200C.
12. Spray a medium-sized baking dish with non-stick spray.

13. Cut away the stem part and cut out seeds of the red and green bell pepper and chop peppers into pieces about an inch across. Line up sausage on a cutting board and cut them into thirds.
14. Put peppers into the baking dish, toss with 1 teaspoon olive oil, sprinkle with Spike Seasoning and fresh-ground black pepper, then add the sausages and stir to combine.
15. Put the dish in the oven and bake 20 minutes, stir and cook for 20 minutes more.
16. Remove from oven, turn oven to BROIL, sprinkle the grated Mozzarella over the sausage-pepper combination and put back in oven and broil 1-2 minutes, or until the cheese is nicely melted and starting to brown.
17. Serve hot.

Nutritional Facts:

- Calories: 321
- Fats: 22g
- Carbohydrates: 7g
- Proteins: 14g

Meat Bagel

Serves: 6

Cook Time: 35 minutes

Ingredients

- 1 ½ onions, finely diced
- 1 tbsp butter/grass fed ghee/bacon fat etc.
- 2 pounds ground pork

- 2 large eggs
- 2/3 cup tomato sauce
- 1 tsp paprika
- 1 tsp sea salt
- 1/2 tsp ground pepper

Directions

1. Preheat the oven to 400 degrees F. Line a baking dish with parchment paper.
2. Sauté the onions over medium heat with some cooking fat, like butter, grass fed ghee etc. Sauté until translucent. Allow the onions to cool before adding them to the meat.
3. In a bowl, mix all of the ingredients including the cooked onions. Mix well enough to evenly distribute the spices.
4. Divide the meat into 6 portions. Using your hands, roll a portion into a ball and then indent the middle, and flatten slightly to form the appearance of a bagel.
5. Place the bagel looking meat in the dish and repeat with each of the portions of meat.
6. Bake for 40 minutes or until the meat is fully cooked.
7. Allow the meat bagels to cool. Slice the meat bagel just like a regular bagel. Fill the meat bagel with topping such as tomato slices, lettuce, onions etc.

Nutritional Facts:

- Calories: 367
- Fats: 30g
- Carbohydrates: 7g
- Proteins: 18g

Fluffy Blueberry Pancakes

Serves: 3

Cook Time: 5 minutes

Ingredients

- 1/2 cup almond flour
- 2 tbsp coconut flour
- 1 tsp cinnamon
- 1/2 tsp baking powder
- 1-2 tbsp granulated sweetener of choice
- 3 large eggs
- 1/4 cup milk of choice
- 1/4 cup blueberries Fresh or thawed frozen ones work best

Directions

1. In a high-speed blender, add your ingredients, except your blueberries, and mix until a thick batter remains.
2. Pour your batter into a large mixing bowl and stir through your blueberries. Let your batter sit for 5-10 minutes, to thicken. If the batter is too thick, add a little milk of choice.
3. Preheat a large non-stick pan over low-medium heat. Ensure the pan is greased. Once hot, Pour 1/4 cup portions of the batter onto the pan and cover immediately. Allow pancakes to cook for 2-3 minutes, until the edges go golden, before flipping and repeating.
4. Once cooked, serve immediately, or cool completely before refrigerating/freezing for later.

Nutritional Facts:

- Calories: 123
- Fats: 7g
- Carbohydrates: 4g
- Proteins: 7g

Steak and Eggs

Serves: 1

Cook Time: 5 minutes

Ingredients

- 1 tbsp butter
- 3 eggs
- 4 oz. sirloin
- 1/4 avocado
- salt
- pepper

Directions

1. Melt your butter in a pan and fry 2-3 eggs until the whites are set and yolk is to desired doneness. Season with salt and pepper.
2. In another pan, cook your sirloin (or favorite cut of steak) until desired doneness. Then slice into bite sized strips and season with salt and pepper.
3. Slice up some avocado and serve together!

Nutritional Facts:

- Calories: 510
- Fats: 36g
- Carbohydrates: 4g
- Proteins: 44g

Creamy Kale and Eggs

Serves: 4

Cook Time: 20 minutes

Ingredients

- 4 large eggs
- Coconut Milk Creamed Spinach
- 2 tablespoons Roasted Red Peppers (jarred or homemade)
- 8 Cherry Tomatoes
- 1/2 cup Grated Mozzarella Cheese optional

Directions

1. Preheat oven to 400 degrees F
2. Butter 4 small, oven proof ramekins and place on a cookie sheet
3. Make a batch of my Coconut Creamed Spinach, using kale instead of Spinach.
4. Add in chopped Roasted Red peppers at the end of cooking.
5. Divide your Creamed Spinach between your ramekins
6. Top each with halved cherry tomatoes and mozzarella cheese if desired
7. Using a spoon create a small indent in the top of each and fill each with an egg & season with salt & pepper.

8. Bake at 400 degrees for 15-20 minutes, just until eggs are cooked but yokes are still runny.
9. Allow to cool slightly before serving
10. Enjoy!

Nutritional Facts:

- Calories: 510
- Fats: 36g
- Carbohydrates: 4g
- Proteins: 44g

Freezer Breakfast Pockets

Serves: 8

Cook Time: 20 minutes

Ingredients

- Dough Ingredients:
- 8 oz mozzarella cheese shredded or cubed
- 2 oz cream cheese
- 2/3 cup almond flour
- 1/3 cup coconut flour
- 1 egg
- 2 tsp baking powder
- 1 tsp salt
- Filling Ingredients:
- 2 eggs scrambled
- 4 oz Canadian bacon or other cooked breakfast meat

- 1/2 cup shredded cheddar cheese or other cheese or your choice

Directions

1. Preheat oven to 350.
2. Put mozzarella cheese and the cream cheese in a microwave-safe bowl. Microwave one minute. Stir. Microwave 30 seconds. Stir. At this point, all the cheese should be melted. Microwave 30 more seconds (it should look like cheese fondue at this point).
3. Put the melted cheese and the other dough ingredients into a food processor and pulse until a uniform dough forms. (Alternatively, you can mix by hand but make sure to knead the dough thoroughly).
4. Divide the dough into 8 pieces. Press each into a 6-inch circle on a piece of parchment paper on a baking sheet. It helps to wet your hands. Divide the filling between each circle of dough. Fold in the edges and crimp to seal. Place back on the parchment seam side down.
5. Bake for 20-25 minutes until golden brown.

Nutritional Facts:

- Calories: 258
- Fats: 18g
- Carbohydrates: 6g
- Proteins: 16g

McMuffin Sausage and Egg Breakfast Sandwich

Serves: 1

Cook Time: 10 minutes

Ingredients

- 1 tbsp butter
- 2 large eggs
- 1 tbsp mayonnaise
- 2 sausage patties, cooked
- 2 slices sharp cheddar cheese
- a few slices of avocado

Directions

1. Heat the butter in a large skillet over medium heat. Place lightly oiled mason jar rings or silicone egg molds into the pan.
2. Crack the eggs into the rings and use a fork to break the yolks and gently whisk. Cover and cook for 3-4 minutes or until eggs are cooked through. Remove the eggs from the rings.
3. Place one of the eggs on a plate and top it with half of the mayonnaise. Top the egg with one of the sausage patties.
4. Top the sausage patty with a slice of cheese and avocado.
5. Put the second sausage patty on top of the avocado and top it with the remaining cheese.
6. Spread the remaining mayonnaise on the second cooked egg and put it on top of the cheese.
7. Serve and enjoy!

Nutritional Facts:

- Calories: 880
- Fats: 82g
- Carbohydrates: 8g
- Proteins: 32g

Broccoli Cheese Breakfast Casserole

Serves: 6

Cook Time: 25 minutes

Ingredients

- 12 eggs, beaten with a fork
- 2 T milk or half and half (probably optional)
- 1 tsp. Spike Seasoning (Or use any all-purpose seasoning that's good with eggs.)
- fresh ground black pepper to taste
- 3 cups broccoli florets
- 1/4 cup grated Swiss cheese
- 1/4 cup grated Mozzarella cheese
- 1/4 cup grated sharp cheddar cheese
- (You can also use 3/4 cup of any grated cheese that you prefer.)
- Optional: sour cream for serving

Directions

1. Preheat oven or toaster oven to 375 degrees. Spray a glass casserole dish with nonstick spray. (I use 7.25 X 11.25 inch pan for this size, but it can be a little larger if you don't have that size.)
2. Cut broccoli into flowerets about 1 inch across.
3. Put broccoli into pot with enough water to cover and bring to a boil. As soon as the water boils and broccoli turns bright green (less than 5 minutes) immediately drain broccoli into colander.
4. While broccoli cools, break eggs into mixing bowl. Add milk or half and half, Spike seasoning, and black pepper and beat eggs until ingredients are well combined.

5. Put the well-drained broccoli into casserole dish. Sprinkle cheeses over broccoli.
6. Pour eggs over broccoli-cheese, then use a fork to gently stir so that broccoli and cheeses are evenly distributed throughout the eggs.
7. Bake at 375 degrees for about 25 minutes, or until top is slightly browned and eggs puff up slightly.
8. Serve hot, with sour cream if desired.
9. This will keep in the fridge for several days and can be reheated in the microwave or in a hot frying pan.

Nutritional Facts:

- Calories: 880
- Fats: 82g
- Carbohydrates: 8g
- Proteins: 32g

Black Forest Mocha Chia Seed Pudding

Serves: 1

Prep Time: 10 minutes

Ingredients

- 1/4 cup (60 ml) heavy cream (or you can sub half & half)
- 3/4 (180 ml) strong brewed coffee, cooled to room temperature
- 3 tablespoons chia seeds
- 2 tablespoons unsweetened cocoa powder
- 1 1/2 teaspoons granulated stevia (see Note)
- 1/2 teaspoon pure vanilla extract

- 1/8 teaspoon pure almond extract
- 1 pinch sea salt
- 10 almonds, toasted and chopped (for garnish)
- 10 cherries, washed, pitted, and halved (for garnish)

Directions

1. Stir together the cream, coffee, chia seeds, cocoa powder, stevia, vanilla extract, almond extract, and salt in a medium bowl. Cover and refrigerate overnight.
2. Puree the mixture in a blender or food processor until smooth.
3. Transfer to 2 serving glasses, top with the almonds and cherries, and serve.

Nutritional Facts:

- Calories: 270
- Fats: 22g
- Carbohydrates: 2g
- Proteins: 6g

2. SNACKS AND DRINKS

Mini Taco Egg Muffins

Serves: 32

Cook Time: 25 minutes

Ingredients

- 1 lb grass-fed ground beef
- 3 tbsp taco seasoning
- 2 tbsp salted butter melted
- 6 large eggs
- 6 ounces Mexican Blend shredded cheese
- 1 cup salsa
- Other garnish such as sour cream, sliced olives or guacamole

Directions

1. In a large skillet over medium heat, sauté the beef until almost cooked through, breaking up the clumps with a wooden spoon. Add the taco seasoning and continue to sauté until completely cooked through. Remove from heat and let cool.
2. Preheat the oven to 350F and brush a good non-stick mini muffin pan with the melted butter. (You can also use silicone or parchment mini muffin liners, if you prefer - if your pan is not very non-stick, this is your best option). This recipe makes about 32 mini muffins so you may need to work in batches if you don't have more than one mini muffin pan.
3. In a large bowl, whisk the eggs. Add the taco meat and 4 ounces of the shredded cheese. Whisk thoroughly to combine.
4. Fill the muffin cups to about ¾ full and sprinkle with the remaining shredded cheese. Bake 15 to 20 minutes, until puffed

and firm to the touch. Remove and let cool 10 minutes. Use a thin flexible spatula to run around the edge of the muffins to release.
5. Serve with your favourite taco toppings, such as salsa, sour cream, and guacamole.

Nutritional Facts:

- Calories: 329
- Fats: 22g
- Carbohydrates: 2g
- Proteins: 25g

Cheesy Garlic Bread Muffins

Serves: 12

Cook Time: 25 minutes

Ingredients

- 6 tbsp butter melted
- 5 cloves garlic pressed or finely minced, divided
- 1/2 cup sour cream
- 4 large eggs
- 1 tsp salt
- 3 cups almond flour
- 2 tsp baking powder
- 1 cup shredded Cheddar cheese I used Cabot Seriously Sharp
- 1/4 cup chopped parsley
- 4 ounces shredded mozzarella
- Sea salt for sprinkling

Directions

1. Preheat the oven to 325F and grease a standard-size non-stick muffin tin very well. Set the muffin tin on a large rimmed baking sheet (to catch the drips).
2. Combine the melted butter and 3 cloves of the garlic. Set aside.
3. In a high-powered blender or a food processor, combine the sour cream, eggs, remaining garlic, and salt. Process until well combined. Add the almond flour, baking powder, cheese, and parsley and process again until smooth.
4. Divide half of the batter between the prepared muffin cups and use a spoon to make a small well in the center of each.
5. Divide the shredded mozzarella between the muffins, pressing into the wells. Drizzle with about 1 tsp of the garlic butter mixture.
6. Divide the remaining batter between each muffin cup, make sure to cover the cheese as best you can. Brush the tops with the remaining garlic butter and sprinkle with sea salt.
7. Bake 25 minutes or so, until tops are golden brown and just firm to the touch. These will drip a lot of oil as they bake and it may spill over the sides a bit (hence the baking sheet underneath - to save your oven!).
8. Remove and let cool 10 minutes before serving. They are fantastic still warm from the oven with the cheese still gooey. They are great cool too and warm up nicely.

Nutritional Facts:

- Calories: 322
- Fats: 27g
- Carbohydrates: 8g
- Proteins: 12g

Buffalo Chicken Sausage Balls

Serves: 12

Cook Time: 25 minutes

Ingredients

- Sausage Balls:
- 2 14-ounce packages al fresco fresh Buffalo-Style chicken sausage casings removed
- 2 cups almond flour
- 1 ½ cups shredded cheddar cheese
- ½ cup crumbled bleu cheese optional
- 1 tsp salt
- ½ tsp pepper
- Bleu Cheese Ranch Dipping Sauce:
- 1/3 cup mayonnaise
- 1/3 cup unsweetened almond milk can substitute regular milk
- 2 cloves garlic minced
- 1 tsp dried dill
- ½ tsp dried parsley
- ½ tsp salt
- ½ tsp pepper
- ¼ cup crumbled bleu cheese or more, if desired

Directions

1. Sausage Balls:
2. Preheat oven to 350F and line two large baking sheets with parchment paper or tin foil.

3. In a large bowl, combine sausage, almond flour, cheddar cheese, bleu cheese, salt and pepper. Mix thoroughly until well combined.
4. Roll into 1-inch balls and place about an inch apart on prepared baking sheets. Bake 25 minutes, until golden brown. Serve warm with dipping sauce.
5. Dipping Sauce:
6. While sausage balls are baking, combine mayonnaise, almond milk, garlic, dill, parsley, salt, and pepper in a medium bowl. Stir well and then mix in crumbled bleu cheese.

Nutritional Facts:

- Calories: 325
- Fats: 25g
- Carbohydrates: 6g
- Proteins: 20g

Corn Dog Nuggets
Serves: 24

Cook Time: 25 minutes

Ingredients

- 2/3 cup coconut flour
- Sweetener of choice equivalent to 2 tbsp sugar
- 1 1/2 tsp baking powder
- 1/4 tsp salt
- 5 large eggs
- 5 tbsp butter, melted
- 3/4 cup almond milk (or use half water, half cream for a nut-free version)

- 1/4 tsp vanilla
- 1 1/2 cups shredded cheddar cheese, divided
- 5 hot dogs, each cut into 6 even pieces

Directions

1. Preheat oven to 325F and grease a non-stick mini muffin pan very well. If you do not have a good non-stick pan, you may want to consider paper liners.
2. In a large bowl, combine coconut flour, sweetener, baking powder, and salt, breaking up any clumps with the back of a fork. Stir in eggs, butter, milk, and vanilla extract until well combined. Stir in 3/4 cup of the shredded cheese.
3. Fill each mini muffin cavity about two thirds full of batter (you may end up with a little too much batter and will need to do another round). Press one piece of hot dog into the center of each. Sprinkle the tops with remaining cheese.
4. Bake 15 to 20 minutes, or until cheese is melted and muffins are firm to the touch. Remove and let cool 15 minutes, then gently run a knife around the edges of each and remove them from the pan.

Nutritional Facts:

- Calories: 260
- Fats: 17g
- Carbohydrates: 7g
- Proteins: 14g

Mini Pizza Muffins

Serves: 16

Cook Time: 25 minutes

Ingredients

- 2 cups almond flour
- 3 tbsp unflavoured whey protein
- 1 tbsp pizza seasoning
- 1 1/2 tsp baking powder
- 1/2 tsp garlic powder
- 1/4 tsp salt
- 1 1/4 cup shredded mozzarella cheese
- 1 cup diced pepperoni
- 2 large eggs
- 5 tbsp butter, melted
- 3/4 cup almond milk

Directions

1. Preheat oven to 325F and grease a mini muffin pan very well or line with paper liners.
2. In a large bowl, whisk together almond flour, whey protein powder, pizza seasoning, baking powder, garlic powder and salt. Stir in cheese and pepperoni.
3. Whisk in eggs, butter and almond milk until well combined. Fill muffin cups about 3/4 full. You will have leftover batter and will need to do a second batch.
4. Bake 17 to 20 minutes, until muffins are golden brown and just firm to the touch. Let cool in pan 10 minutes, then transfer to a wire rack to cool completely.

5. Repeat with remaining batter. Serve with no sugar added marinara sauce.

Nutritional Facts:

- Calories: 184
- Fats: 14g
- Carbohydrates: 3g
- Proteins: 8g

Rosemary Parmesan Crackers

Serves: 40

Cook Time: 45 minutes

Ingredients

- 1 1/2 cups Bob's Red Mill raw sunflower seeds
- 1/2 cup Bob's Red Mill chia seeds
- 3/4 cup finely grated Parmesan
- 2 tbsp chopped fresh rosemary
- 1/2 tsp garlic powder
- 1/2 tsp baking powder
- 1 large egg
- 2 tbsp melted butter
- 1/2 tsp kosher salt

Directions

1. Preheat oven to 300F.

2. In a high-powered blender or food processor, grind the sunflower seeds and chia seeds until finely ground (I actually grind mine in batches in my coffee grinder, it works quite well). Then measure out 1 1/2 cups of the ground sunflower seeds and 1/2 cup of the ground chia seeds into a large bowl.
3. Stir in Parmesan, fresh rosemary, garlic powder and baking powder.
4. Stir in egg and butter until dough comes together.
5. Turn dough out onto a large piece of parchment paper and pat into a rough triangle. Top with another large piece of parchment paper. Roll out to about a 1/8-inch thickness, as evenly as you can. Remove top parchment
6. Use a sharp knife or pizza cutter to score into 2 inch squares. Sprinkle with kosher salt. Transfer whole bottom parchment paper to a large baking sheet.
7. Bake 40 to 45 minutes, or until edges are golden brown and the crackers are firm to the touch. Remove and let cool completely before breaking apart. They will continue to crisp up as they cool (but I don't blame you for breaking off the uneven edges and nibbling on those!)

Nutritional Facts:

- Calories: 223
- Fats: 18g
- Carbohydrates: 8g
- Proteins: 8g

Mini Pepper Nachos

Serves: 6

Cook Time: 20 minutes

Ingredients

- 1 tbsp chili powder
- 1 tsp ground cumin
- 1 tsp garlic powder
- 1 tsp paprika
- 1/2 tsp kosher salt
- 1/2 tsp pepper
- 1/2 tsp oregano
- 1/4 tsp red pepper flakes (more if you like it hotter)
- 1 lb ground beef
- 1 lb mini peppers, halved and seeded
- 1 1/2 cups shredded Cheddar cheese
- 1/2 cup chopped tomato
- Other toppings as desired (sour cream, olives, chopped jalapeño, avocado, etc.)

Directions

1. In a small bowl, combine chili powder, cumin, garlic powder, paprika, salt, pepper, oregano and red pepper flakes.
2. In a large skillet over medium heat, brown ground beef until just cooked through, about 7 to 10 minutes, breaking up any clumps with the back of a wooden spoon. Add spice mixture and sauté until well combined. Remove from heat.
3. Preheat oven to 400F and line a large baking try with parchment paper or aluminum foil. Arrange mini peppers in a single layer, cut-side up but very close together.

4. Sprinkle with ground beef mixture and shredded cheese (make sure every mini pepper gets a little meat and cheese!). Bake 5 to 10 minutes, until cheese is melty.
5. Remove from oven and top with chopped tomatoes and any other desired toppings. Serve immediately.

Nutritional Facts:

- Calories: 351
- Fats: 21g
- Carbohydrates: 6g
- Proteins: 28g

Iced Apple Green Tea

Serves: 2

Prep Time: 2 minutes

Ingredients

- 1 cup (240 ml) of brewed green tea
- 1 cup (240 g) ice
- 1 teaspoon (5 ml) apple cider vinegar
- Stevia, to taste

Directions

1. Brew the green tea with hot water for 2-3 minutes.
2. Add all the ingredients to a blender and blend well.

Nutritional Facts:

- Calories: 10
- Fats: 0g
- Carbohydrates: 0g
- Proteins: 0g

Bloody Mary

Serves: 2

Prep Time: 5 minutes

Ingredients

- 4 ounces unsweetened tomato vegetable juice
- 2 ounces vodka
- 1 teaspoon Worcestershire sauce
- 2 teaspoons (or more) prepared horseradish
- 1/4 teaspoon smoked tobasco sauce
- 1/2 teaspoon granulated sugar substitute
- 1/8 teaspoon powdered beef boullion (optional)
- 1/2 teaspoon ground black pepper
- 1 teaspoon fresh lemon juice

Directions

1. Combine all of the ingredients in a cocktail shaker with 5 cubes of ice.
2. Shake well.
3. Strain into a 10 ounce highball glass filled with ice.
4. Garnish with celery, chilled cooked shrimp, olives, and/or cooked bacon as desired.

Nutritional Facts:

- Calories: 163
- Fats: 0g
- Carbohydrates: 7g
- Proteins: 1g

Homemade Coffee Liqueur

Serves: 20

Prep Time: 15 minutes

Ingredients

- Coffee Liqueur
- 2 cups water
- 3/4 cup Swerve Sweetener
- 1/8 tsp monk fruit extract or another 1/2 cup Swerve
- 1/4 cup ground coffee I used decaf
- 1 1/2 cup vodka
- 1 tbsp cocoa powder
- 1 tsp vanilla extract
- Mexican Coffee:
- 1 oz coffee liqueur
- 1/2 oz tequila if you're feeling bold. If not, feel free to add a touch more coffee liqueur or vodka
- 1 cup freshly brewed coffee
- 3 tablespoons whipped cream
- sprinkle of cinnamon

Directions

1. For the liqueur: In a medium saucepan over medium-high heat, combine water, erythritol, monk fruit extract, and coffee grounds.
2. Bring to a boil, then reduce heat and simmer for 10 minutes. Let cool.
3. Transfer mixture to a glass jar and add vodka, cocoa powder and vanilla extract
4. Seal jar and place in a dark, cool spot and wait...and wait...and wait. At least 3 weeks, shaking the jar every few days.
5. Strain mixture through a fine mesh sieve. Then strain again through a coffee filter (this will take several day and changes of coffee filter, but it's worth it to get all the coffee "silt" out of the mixture).
6. For the Mexican Coffee, mix liqueur, tequila and coffee in a large coffee mug. Top with whipped cream and cinnamon.

Nutritional Facts:

- Calories: 42
- Fats: 0g
- Carbohydrates: 1g
- Proteins: 0g

Minty Moscow Mule

Serves: 2

Prep Time: 5 minutes

Ingredients

- For the Ginger Syrup:
- 1/2 cup thinly sliced, peeled ginger
- 2 cups water
- 1/3 cup granulated sugar substitute (I used Swerve)
- For the Moscow Mule:

- 4 oz premium vodka
- 1 oz fresh lime juice
- 1 oz ginger syrup (recipe above)
- 8 oz diet ginger ale
- fresh mint leaves to garnish

Directions

1. For the Ginger Syrup:
2. Combine the ginger, water and sweetener in a small saucepan.
3. Bring to a boil over high heat. Lower the heat to medium and simmer for 10 minutes.
4. Cool for 1 hour, then strain and store in a clean jar in the fridge for up to 2 weeks.
5. For the Moscow Mules:
6. Combine the vodka, lime juice, ginger syrup and ginger ale in a small pitcher. Stir well.
7. Pour over ice and garnish with fresh mint. For a stronger mint flavor, muddle (smash) the mint leaves around in the bottom of the mug slightly before drinking.

Nutritional Facts:

- Calories: 134
- Fats: 0g
- Carbohydrates: 1g
- Proteins: 0g

Boozy Root beer Float

Serves: 1

Prep Time: 2 minutes

Ingredients

- 1/2 cup low carb vanilla ice cream
- 2 ounces vanilla flavored vodka
- 12 ounces diet vanilla root beer

Directions

1. Place your ice cream in a tall glass
2. Pour the soda and vodka into a container with a lip for pouring and stir slightly to mix.
3. Pour the vodka and soda mixture slowly over the ice cream. You may have to do this in stages to let the bubbles recede. Let it sit for 2 minutes before drinking.

Nutritional Facts:

- Calories: 258
- Fats: 6g
- Carbohydrates: 4g
- Proteins: 2g

3. SOUPS AND SALADS

Roasted Tomato & Garlic Soup

Serves: 4

Cook Time: 40 minutes

Ingredients

- 1 lb fresh tomatoes, cored
- 4 cloves garlic, peeled
- 2 tablespoons olive oil
- 1/2 teaspoon kosher salt
- 1/4 teaspoon ground black pepper
- 4 cups chicken broth
- 2 tablespoons olive oil
- 1/8th teaspoon ground nutmeg
- 1/4 teaspoon anchovy paste
- 2 bay leaves
- 1 teaspoon apple cider vinegar
- Salt and pepper to taste

Directions

1. Preheat the oven to 400 degrees.
2. Place the cored tomatoes and peeled garlic on a cookie sheet.
3. Drizzle with 2 tablespoons of olive oil, salt and pepper.
4. Roast for 30 minutes.
5. Remove and transfer vegetables and any pan juices to a blender.
6. Add 2 cups of chicken stock and blend until smooth.
7. Pour through a strainer (to remove seeds and skin pieces) into a large saucepan.

8. Add the remaining 2 cups of chicken stock, 2 tablespoons olive oil, nutmeg, anchovy paste and bay leaves.
9. Simmer over medium heat for 10 minutes.
10. Remove the bay leaves.
11. Add apple cider vinegar.
12. Stir and taste, season with additional salt and pepper as desired.

Nutritional Facts:

- Calories: 130
- Fats: 11g
- Carbohydrates: 6g
- Proteins: 2g

Easy Low Carb Chicken Soup

Serves: 8

Cook Time: 40 minutes

Ingredients

- 10 cups bone broth or chicken stock
- 1/2 tsp garlic powder
- 1/2 tsp dried oregano
- 1 cup thinly sliced celery
- 1 1/2 cups diced butternut squash
- 2 cups jicama, peeled and chopped small into "rice"
- 4 cups cooked, shredded or chopped chicken
- 1/4 cup chopped fresh parsley
- 1 Tbsp apple cider vinegar
- sea salt and pepper to taste

Directions

1. Combine the broth, garlic powder, dried oregano, celery, butternut squash and jicama in a large pot.
2. Bring to a boil, then lower heat and simmer (uncovered) for 30 minutes, or until veggies are fork tender.
3. Add the chicken and cook for another 5 minutes, or until heated through (don't cook the chicken too long or it will get tough.)
4. Remove from the heat and add the parsley and apple cider vinegar.
5. Season with sea salt and pepper to taste before serving.

Nutritional Facts:

- Calories: 190
- Fats: 5g
- Carbohydrates: 5g
- Proteins: 26g

Poblano Chicken Soup

Serves: 8

Cook Time: 40 minutes

Ingredients

- 1/2 cup navy beans soaked for an hour in hot water
- 1 cup onion diced
- 3 poblano peppers chopped
- 5 cloves Garlic
- 1 cup cauliflower diced
- 1.5 pounds chicken breast, large chunks
- 1/4 cup cilantro chopped

- 1 teaspoon Ground Coriander
- 1 teaspoon Ground Cumin
- 1-2 teaspoons Salt
- For Finishing
- 2 ounces cream cheese

Directions

1. Put everything except the cream cheese into your Instant Pot, and cook at high pressure for 15 minutes. Allow it to release pressure naturally for ten minutes, and the release all remaining pressure.
2. Remove chicken with tongs and using an immersion blender, roughly purée the soup and vegetables.
3. Turn your pot onto Sauté, and when the broth is hot and bubbling, put in the cream cheese cut into chunks. Use a whisk to blend in the cream cheese if needed.
4. Shred the chicken and put back into the pot, until heated through.
5. You can also purée the vegetables and chicken together, to get a thicker, more robust soup.

Nutritional Facts:

- Calories: 190
- Fats: 5g
- Carbohydrates: 13g
- Proteins: 22g

Hearty Ham and Green Bean Soup

Serves: 12

Cook Time: 30 minutes

Ingredients

- 1 quart ham broth
- 1 quart chicken broth
- 2 cups water
- 2 tablespoons bacon drippings
- 2 cloves garlic (chopped)
- 3 ounces onion (chopped)
- 1 pound green beans cut into 1 inch pieces
- 1 pound red potatoes (cubed)
- 1 pound ham (cubed)
- 1/2 teaspoon garlic powder
- 1 teaspoon salt
- 1/2 teaspoon liquid smoke flavoring
- salt and pepper to taste

Directions

1. Chop the onion and garlic. Put the bacon drippings or oil in a large soup pot and heat on medium heat. Saute the onions and garlic in the oil until they are translucent. While the onions are cooking, chop the potatoes into bite sized pieces. If you aren't using left over green beans, then cut the green beans, too.
2. Pour the ham and chicken broths into the pot with the water and bring up to a low boil. Skim any foam that forms at the top of the soup. Add green beans and cook for a few minutes. Then add the

potatoes, salt, liquid smoke flavoring and garlic powder. Simmer gently until the potatoes are cooked though. Add the ham and heat through. Adjust the seasonings and serve.

Nutritional Facts:

- Calories: 158
- Fats: 7g
- Carbohydrates: 12g
- Proteins: 11g

Creamy Pumpkin & Sausage Chowder

Serves: 8

Cook Time: 30 minutes

Ingredients

- 1 pound pork sausage roll (usually found with breakfast meats)
- 4 cups chicken broth
- 1 1/4 cup solid pack pumpkin puree
- 3 cups water
- 1/4 cup dry sherry
- 1 teaspoon kosher salt
- 1/4 teaspoon ground nutmeg
- 1/4 teaspoon ground black pepper
- 1 teaspoon garlic powder
- 1 teaspoon onion powder
- 3 cups cauliflower rice

- 1 tablespoon minced fresh sage
- 8 ounces mascarpone cheese

Directions

1. Brown the sausage in a large saucepan, stirring to break it up into small pieces.
2. Add the chicken broth, pumpkin puree, water, sherry, salt, nutmeg, pepper, garlic, onion, and cauliflower. Simmer 20 minutes.
3. Add the mascarpone cheese and sage. Cook over medium low heat, stirring occasionally, for five minutes or until the cheese has melted into the broth and is creamy and smooth. Do not boil.
4. Serve hot.
5. Store leftovers in an airtight container in the refrigerator for up to 5 days.

Nutritional Facts:

- Calories: 308
- Fats: 25g
- Carbohydrates: 7g
- Proteins: 9g

Tomato Basil Soup

Serves: 6

Cook Time: 20 minutes

Ingredients

- 1 can (28 ounces) whole plum tomatoes (San Marzano preferred)
- 2 cups filtered water
- 1.5 teaspoons coarse kosher salt
- 1/2 teaspoon onion powder
- 1/4 teaspoon garlic powder
- 1 tablespoon butter
- 8 ounces mascarpone cheese
- 2 tablespoons granulated erythritol sweetener
- 1 teaspoon apple cider vinegar
- 1/4 teaspoon dried basil leaves
- 1/4 cup prepared basil pesto, plus more for garnish if desired

Directions

1. Combine the canned tomatoes, water, salt, onion powder and garlic powder in a medium saucepan.
2. Bring to a boil over medium-high heat and then simmer for 2 minutes.
3. Remove from the heat and puree with an immersion blender until smooth (or transfer to a traditional blender and blend, then return blended soup to the pan.)
4. Return to the stove and add the butter and mascarpone cheese to the soup.
5. Stir over low heat until melted and creamy – about 2 minutes.
6. Remove from the heat and stir in the sweetener, apple cider vinegar, dried basil, and pesto.
7. Serve warm.

8. Store any leftovers in a covered container in the refrigerator for up to 5 days, or in the freezer for up to three months.

Nutritional Facts:

- Calories: 258
- Fats: 23g
- Carbohydrates: 7g
- Proteins: 4g

Southwestern Pumpkin Cheddar Soup

Serves: 6

Cook Time: 4 Hours

Ingredients

- 1/2 onion minced
- 15 ounce can pumpkin puree
- 4 cups chicken broth preferably homemade
- 1/2 tsp salt
- 1/2 tsp cumin
- 1/2 tsp garlic powder
- 1/4 tsp chipotle powder or more to taste, if you like it spicy. We do!
- 1/4 tsp black pepper
- 6 ounces sharp cheddar cheese grated (I recommend Cabot Farmhouse Reserve)
- 1 lb chorizo or other spicy sausage cooked and crumbled

- Salt and pepper to taste

Directions

1. Add onion, pumpkin puree, chicken broth, salt, cumin, garlic powder, chipotle powder and pepper to a large slow cooker. Stir well and cook on low for 4 hours or on high for 2 hours.
2. Add shredded cheese and let melt, then blend soup with an immersion blender or transfer to a large blender or food processor (you may need to work in batches).
3. Spoon into bowls and sprinkle each with chorizo.
4. You can also make this recipe on the stove, in a large saucepan or stockpot. Simply simmer the ingredients from the first step for 20 minutes or so before adding the cheese and blending.

Nutritional Facts:

- Calories: 457
- Fats: 34g
- Carbohydrates: 10g
- Proteins: 20g

BLT Lobster Roll Salad

Serves: 4

Prep Time: 10 minutes

Ingredients

- For the lobster salad:
- 2 cups cooked lobster meat, chopped into bite sized pieces
- 1 1/2 cups cauliflower florets, cooked until tender and chilled
- 1/2 cup sugar free mayonnaise
- 1 tsp fresh tarragon leaves, chopped
- To serve:
- 8 fresh romaine lettuce leaves
- 1/2 cup chopped tomatoes
- 1/2 cup cooked bacon, chopped

Directions

1. For the salad:
2. Combine the cooked lobster, cooked cauliflower, mayonnaise and tarragon in a medium bowl. Stir until well combined and creamy.
3. To serve:
4. Lay the lettuce leaves on a platter. Divide the lobster salad mixture between the 8 leaves. Sprinkle with chopped tomatoes and chopped bacon.
5. Serve cold or at room temperature.

Nutritional Facts:

- Calories: 330
- Fats: 28g
- Carbohydrates: 3g
- Proteins: 20g

Amish Broccoli Cauliflower Salad

Serves: 7

Prep Time: 20 minutes

Ingredients

- Salad
- 8 oz broccoli florets, cut into bite-sized pieces
- 8 oz cauliflower florets, cut into bite-sized pieces
- 2 oz red bell pepper (1/2 of a pepper), small dice
- 4 oz cheddar cheese, cubed
- 1/3 pound bacon, cooked crisp and crumbled
- 2 tbsp purple onion (or green onion)
- Dressing
- 3/4 cup mayonnaise
- 3/4 cup sour cream (or full-fat Greek yogurt)
- 2 tbsp Sukrin Melis Icing Sugar (or Swerve Confectioners or stevia to taste)*
- 1 tbsp fresh lemon juice

Directions

1. Preparation
2. Dice bacon and cook it in a frying pan over medium heat until crisp, about 6 minutes. Drain. (If serving the salad the next day, store separately.)
3. Meanwhile, wash and chop the vegetables and place into a large bowl. If serving the salad the next day, cover and refrigerate.
4. Mix the ingredients for the dressing in a medium bowl and taste to adjust the seasoning. Cover and refrigerate if not using right away.
5. Assemble

6. Toss the salad ingredients with the broccoli then stir in the dressing. (I use less dressing than the recipe makes - as shown in the photos, but you may want to use it all.) Serve.
7. Refrigerate any leftovers up to 5 days. Makes 7 cups at 1 cup per serving.

Nutritional Facts:

- Calories: 324
- Fats: 32g
- Carbohydrates: 5g
- Proteins: 7g

Grilled Chicken & Baby Bok Choy Salad

Serves: 4

Prep Time: 10 minutes

Ingredients

- For the salad:
- 2 cups grilled chicken, chopped
- 6 baby bok choy, grilled & chopped
- 1/2 cup raw jicama, chopped
- 2 green onions, chopped
- 1/4 cup cilantro, chopped
- 1 Tbsp sesame seeds
- For the dressing:
- 1 Tbsp fresh ginger, chopped

- 2 Tbsp coconut cream
- 1/2 tsp sriracha hot sauce
- 1 Tbsp fish sauce
- 1 Tbsp soy sauce
- 1 Tbsp sesame oil
- 2 Tbsp fresh lime juice
- 1 tsp stevia powder

Directions

1. Combine all of the salad ingredients until well mixed.
2. Add all of the ingredients for the dressing into a blender or food processor, and blend until mostly smooth – there may be some small chunks of ginger left, that's ok. Pour the dressing over the salad and toss lightly until coated.
3. Garnish with more sesame seeds if desired.

Nutritional Facts:

- Calories: 154
- Fats: 7g
- Carbohydrates: 4g
- Proteins: 17g

Creamy Shrimp & Cauliflower Salad

Serves: 8

Prep Time: 10 minutes

Ingredients

- For the salad:
- 5 cups cauliflower florets, cooked and chilled
- 2 cups cooked large shrimp (approx. 1 lb) chilled and cut in half lenthwise
- 1/3 cup diced celery
- 1/2 cup sliced canned black olives
- 1 Tbsp fresh dill, chopped
- For the dressing:
- 1/2 cup mayonnaise
- 1/4 tsp celery seed
- 2 Tbsp lemon juice
- 2 tsp granulated sugar substitute
- 1 tsp apple cider vinegar
- 1/4 tsp kosher salt
- 1/8 tsp ground black pepper

Directions

1. Combine the salad ingredients in a large bowl and toss gently.
2. Combine the dressing ingredients in a small bowl and whisk together until smooth.
3. Pour the dressing over the salad and stir gently until well coated.
4. Chill for half an hour if possible to let the flavors meld.
5. Serve cold.

Nutritional Facts:

- Calories: 182
- Fats: 14g
- Carbohydrates: 2g
- Proteins: 13g

Caprese Zucchini Noodle Pasta Salad

Serves: 8

Prep Time: 15 minutes

Ingredients

- 4 zucchini or 8 cups zucchini noodles
- 4 ounces cherry tomatoes sliced in half
- 8 ounces mozzarella pearls
- 1 ounce fresh basil chopped
- Dressing
- 1/4 cup extra virgin olive oil
- 3 tbsp red wine vinegar
- 1 tbsp lemon juice fresh
- 1/2 tsp salt
- 1/4 tsp pepper
- 1/4 tsp garlic powder

Directions

1. Add all ingredients into a bowl.

2. Whisk dressing ingredients in another bowl and toss together.
3. Enjoy immediately or refrigerate until ready to serve.

Nutritional Facts:

- Calories: 166
- Fats: 14g
- Carbohydrates: 4g
- Proteins: 7g

4. DESSERT

Caramel Cake

Serves: 12

Cook Time: 35 minutes

Ingredients

- 2 1/2 cups almond flour
- 1/4 cup coconut flour
- 1/4 cup unflavored whey protein powder
- 1 tbsp baking powder
- 1/2 tsp salt
- 1/2 cup butter softened
- 2/3 cup Swerve Sweetener
- 4 large eggs room temperature
- 1 tsp vanilla extract
- 3/4 cup almond milk
- 2 batches sugar free caramel sauce

Directions

1. Cake:
2. Preheat the oven to 325F and grease 2 8-inch round cake pans. Cut parchment to line the bottoms of the pans and grease the parchment as well.
3. In a medium bowl, whisk together the almond flour, coconut flour, whey protein, baking powder, and salt.
4. In a large bowl, beat the butter and sweetener together until light and fluffy. Beat in the eggs one at a time and scrape down the beaters and bowl as necessary. Beat in the vanilla extract
5. Add the dry ingredients in two additions, alternating with the almond milk. Beat until well combined.

6. Divide the batter between the two cake pans and spread to the edges. Smooth the tops and bake 25 minutes, or until the edges are golden and the tops are firm to the touch.
7. Remove and let cool in the pans, then flip out onto a wire rack. Be sure to peel off the parchment paper if it sticks to the cake layers.
8. Caramel Glaze:
9. Prepare a double batch of the Sugar Free Caramel Sauce but DO NOT add the additional water at the end of the recipe. Be sure to use a large saucepan (at least 3 quarts) as it will bubble up quite a bit.
10. Let the sauce cool down to room temperature. It should be quite thick at this point, but still pourable, and it will continue to thicken as it cools.
11. Place one layer of cake on a serving plate and pour about 1/3 of the caramel sauce on top. Carefully spread to the edges with an offset spatula and let sit another 10 to 15 minutes to thicken further.
12. Place the second layer of cake on top. Pour some of the caramel over the top, letting it drip down the sides, spreading it over the top and sides as you go. Continue until the top and sides are well covered. Alternatively, you can simply let it drip down the sides and not spread it over.
13. ***If your caramel is too thin and is dripping too much off the sides of the cake, you can whisk in a tablespoon or two of powdered Swerve to help thicken it up. If it gets too thick, you can gently re-warm it over low heat to thin it up again.

Nutritional Facts:

- Calories: 388
- Fats: 35g
- Carbohydrates: 7g
- Proteins: 10g

Classic New York Keto Cheesecake

Serves: 12

Cook Time: 1 Hour 15 minutes

Ingredients

- 24 ounces cream cheese softened
- 5 tbsp unsalted butter softened
- 1 cup powdered Swerve Sweetener
- 3 large eggs room temperature
- 3/4 cup sour cream room temperature
- 2 tsp grated lemon zest
- 1 1/2 tsp vanilla extract

Directions

1. Preheat the oven to 300F and generously grease a 9-inch springform pan. Cut a circle of parchment to fit the bottom the pan and grease the paper. Wrap 2 pieces of aluminum foil around the outside of the pan to cover the bottom and most of the way up the sides.
2. In a large bowl, beat the cream cheese and butter until smooth, then beat in the sweetener until well combined. Add the eggs, once at a time, beating after each addition. Clean the beaters and scrape down the sides of the bowl as needed.
3. Add the sour cream, lemon zest, and vanilla extract and beat until the batter is smooth and well combined. Pour into the prepared springform pan and smooth the top.
4. Set the pan inside a roasting pan large enough to prevent the sides from touching. Place the roasting pan in the oven and carefully pour boiling water into the roasting pan until it reaches halfway up the sides of the springform pan.
5. Bake 70 to 90 minutes, until the cheesecake is mostly set but still jiggles just a little in the center when shaken. Remove the roasting

pan from the one, then carefully remove the springform pan from the water bath. Let cool to room temperature.
6. Run a sharp knife around the edges of the cake to loosen, the release the sides of the pan. Refrigerate for at least 4 hours before serving.

Nutritional Facts:

- Calories: 287
- Fats: 24g
- Carbohydrates: 3g
- Proteins: 6g

Cinnamon Roll Coffee Cake

Serves: 16

Cook Time: 35 minutes

Ingredients

- Cinnamon Filling:
- 3 tbsp Swerve Sweetener
- 2 tsp ground cinnamon
- Cake:
- 3 cups almond flour
- 3/4 cup Swerve Sweetener
- 1/4 cup unflavoured whey protein powder
- 2 tsp baking powder
- 1/2 tsp salt

- 3 large eggs
- 1/2 cup butter melted
- 1/2 tsp vanilla extract
- 1/2 cup almond milk
- 1 tbsp melted butter
- Cream Cheese Frosting:
- 3 tbsp cream cheese softened
- 2 tbsp powdered Swerve Sweetener
- 1 tbsp heavy whipping cream
- 1/2 tsp vanilla extract

Directions

1. Preheat oven to 325F and grease an 8x8 inch baking pan.
2. For the filling, combine the Swerve and cinnamon in a small bowl and mix well. Set aside.
3. For the cake, whisk together almond flour, sweetener, protein powder, baking powder, and salt in a medium bowl.
4. Stir in the eggs, melted butter and vanilla extract. Add the almond milk and continue to stir until well combined.
5. Spread half of the batter in the prepared pan, then sprinkle with about two thirds of the cinnamon filling mixture. Spread the remaining batter over top and smooth with a knife or an offset spatula.
6. Bake 35 minutes, or until top is golden brown and a tester inserted in the center comes out with a few crumbs attached.
7. Brush with melted butter and sprinkle with remaining cinnamon filling mixture. Let cool in pan.
8. For the frosting, beat cream cheese, powdered erythritol, cream and vanilla extract together in a small bowl until smooth. Pipe or drizzle over cooled cake.

Nutritional Facts:

- Calories: 222
- Fats: 20g
- Carbohydrates: 5g
- Proteins: 7g

Chocolate Walnut Torte

Serves: 1

Cook Time: 30 minutes

Ingredients

- Torte:
- 1 1/2 cup walnuts
- 3/4 cup Swerve Sweetener
- 1/4 cup cocoa powder
- 1 tsp espresso powder (optional, enhances chocolate flavour)
- 1/2 tsp baking powder
- 1/4 tsp salt
- 1/2 cup butter
- 4 ounces unsweetened chocolate
- 5 large eggs
- 1/2 tsp vanilla extract
- 1/2 cup almond milk
- Glaze:
- 1/2 cup whipping cream
- 2 1/2 ounces sugar-free dark chocolate chopped
- 1/3 cup walnut pieces

Directions

1. Torte:
2. Preheat oven to 325F and grease a 9-inch round baking pan. Line the bottom with parchment paper and grease the paper.
3. In a food processor, process walnuts until finely ground. Add sweetener, cocoa powder, espresso powder, baking powder, and salt and pulse a few times to combine.
4. In a large saucepan set over low heat, melt butter and chocolate together until smooth. Remove from heat and whisk in eggs and vanilla extract. Add almond milk and whisk until mixture smooths out. Stir in walnut mixture until well combined.
5. Spread batter in prepared baking pan and bake about 30 minutes, until edges are set but center still looks slightly wet. Let cool 15 minutes in pan, then invert onto a wire rack to cool completely. Remove parchment paper.
6. Glaze:
7. In a small saucepan over medium heat, bring cream to just a simmer. Remove from heat and add chopped chocolate. Let sit to melt 5 minutes, then whisk until smooth.
8. Cool another 10 minutes, then pour the glaze over the cake, smoothing the sides. Sprinkle top with walnut pieces and chill until chocolate is firm, about 30 minutes.

Nutritional Facts:

- Calories: 343
- Fats: 30g
- Carbohydrates: 8g
- Proteins: 10g

Kentucky Butter Cake

Serves: 16

Cook Time: 60 minutes

Ingredients

- Cake:
- 2 1/2 cups almond flour
- 1/4 cup coconut flour
- 1/4 cup unflavoured whey protein powder
- 1 tbsp baking powder
- 1/2 tsp salt
- 1 cup butter softened
- 1 cup Swerve Granular
- 5 large eggs room temperature.
- 2 tsp vanilla extract
- 1/2 cup whipping cream
- 1/2 cup water
- Butter Glaze:
- 5 tbsp butter
- 1/3 cup Swerve Granular
- 2 tbsp water
- 1 tsp vanilla extract
- Garnish
- 1 to 2 tbsp Confectioner's Swerve

Directions

1. Preheat oven to 325F. Grease a bundt cake pan VERY well and then dust with a few tbsp of almond flour.
2. In a medium bowl, whisk together the almond flour, coconut flour, whey protein, baking powder, and salt.

3. In a large bowl, beat the butter and the sweetener together until light and creamy. Beat in the eggs and vanilla extract. Beat in the almond flour mixture and then beat in the whipping cream and water until well combined.
4. Transfer the batter to the prepared baking pan and smooth the top. Bake 50 to 60 minutes, until golden brown and the cake is firm to the touch. A tester inserted in the center should come out clean.
5. Butter Glaze: In a small saucepan over low heat, melt the butter and sweetener together. Whisk until well combined. Whisk in the water and vanilla extract.
6. While the cake is still warm and in the pan, poke holes all over with a skewer. Pour the glaze over and let cool completely in the pan.
7. Gently loosen the sides with a knife or thin rubber spatula, then flip out onto a serving platter. Dust with powdered sweetener.
8. Serve with lightly sweetened whipped cream and fresh berries.

Nutritional Facts:

- Calories: 301
- Fats: 27g
- Carbohydrates: 6g
- Proteins: 7g

Pecan Pie Cheesecake

Serves: 10

Cook Time: 35 minutes

Ingredients

- Crust
- 3/4 cup almond flour
- 2 tbsp powdered Swerve Sweetener
- Pinch salt
- 2 tbsp melted butter
- Pecan Pie Filling
- 1/4 cup butter
- 1/3 cup powdered Swerve Sweetener
- 1 tsp Yacon syrup or molasses optiona, for colour and flavour
- 1 tsp caramel extract or vanilla extract
- 2 tbsp heavy whipping cream
- 1 large egg
- 1/4 tsp salt
- 1/2 cup chopped pecans
- Cheesecake Filling
- 12 ounces cream cheese softened
- 5 tbsp powdered Swerve Sweetener
- 1 large egg
- 1/4 cup heavy whipping cream
- 1/2 tsp vanilla extract
- Topping
- 2 tbsp butter
- 2 1/2 tbsp powdered Swerve Sweetener
- 1/2 tsp Yacon syrup or molasses

- 1/2 tsp caramel extract or vanilla extract
- 1 tbsp heavy whipping cream
- Whole toasted pecans for garnish

Directions

1. Crust:
2. In a medium bowl, whisk together the almond flour, sweetener, and salt. Stir in the melted butter until the mixture begins to clump together.
3. Press into the bottom and partway up the sides of a 7-inch springform pan. Place in the freezer while making the pecan pie filling.
4. Pecan Pie Filling:
5. In a small saucepan over low heat, melt the butter. Add the sweetener and Yacon syrup and whisk until combined, then stir in the extract and heavy whipping cream.
6. Add the egg and continue to cook over low heat until the mixture thickens (this should only take a minute or so). Immediately remove from heat and stir in the pecans and salt.
7. Spread mixture over the bottom of the crust.
8. Cheesecake Filling:
9. Beat the cream cheese until smooth, then beat in the sweetener. Beat in the egg, whipping cream, and vanilla a extract.
10. Pour this mixture over the pecan pie filling and spread to the edges.
11. To Bake:
12. Wrap the bottom of the springform pan tightly in a large piece of foil. Place a piece of paper towel over the top of the springform pan (not touching the cheesecake) and then wrap foil around the top as well. Your whole pan should be mostly covered in foil to keep out excess moisture.
13. Place the rack that came with your Instant Pot or pressure cooker into the bottom. Pour a cup of water into the bottom.

14. Carefully lower the wrapped cheesecake pan onto the rack (there are ways to do this with a sling made out of tin foil but I didn't bother with that).
15. Close the lid and set the Instant Pot to manual mode for 30 minutes on high. Once the cooking time is complete, let the pressure to release naturally (do not vent it).
16. Lift out the cheesecake and let it cool to room temperature, and then refrigerate for 3 or 4 hours, or even overnight.
17. Topping:
18. In a small saucepan over low heat, melt the butter. Add the sweetener and Yacon syrup and whisk until combined, then stir in the extract and heavy whipping cream.
19. Drizzle over the chilled cheesecake and garnish with toasted pecans.

Nutritional Facts:

- Calories: 340
- Fats: 31g
- Carbohydrates: 5g
- Proteins: 5g

Gingerbread Cake Roll

Serves: 12

Cook Time: 15 minutes

Ingredients

- Cake
- 1 cup almond flour
- 1/4 cup powdered Swerve Sweetener
- 2 tbsp cocoa powder
- 1 tbsp grassfed gelatin
- 2 tsp ground ginger
- 1 tsp ground cinnamon
- 1/4 tsp ground cloves
- 4 large eggs room temperature, separated
- 1/4 cup granulated Swerve Sweetener divided
- 1 tsp vanilla extract
- 1/4 tsp salt divided
- 1/4 tsp cream of tartar
- Vanilla Cream Filling:
- 2 ounces cream cheese softened
- 1 1/2 cups whipping cream divided
- 1/4 cup powdered Swerve Sweetener
- 1/2 tsp vanilla extract

Directions

1. Cake:
2. Preheat oven to 350F and line an 11x17 inch rimmed baking sheet with parchment paper. Grease the parchment paper and pan sides very well.
3. In a medium bowl, whisk together the almond flour, powdered sweetener, cocoa powder, gelatin, ginger, cinnamon, and cloves.

4. In another medium bowl, beat the egg yolks with 2 tbsp of the granulated sweetener until lighter yellow and thickened. Beat in the vanilla extract
5. Using clean beaters and a large clean bowl, beat the egg whites with the salt and cream of tartar until frothy. Beat in the remaining two tbsp sweetener until stiff peaks form.
6. Gently fold the egg yolk mixture into the whites. Then gently fold in the almond flour mixture, taking care not to deflate them, until no streaks remain.
7. Spread the batter evenly into the prepared baking pan and bake 10 to 12 minutes, until the top springs back when touched.
8. Remove from the oven and let let cool a few minutes, then run a knife around the edges to loosen. Cover with another large piece of parchment paper and then a kitchen towel. Place another large baking sheet overtop and flip over.
9. Gently peel the parchment from what is now the top of the cake. While still warm, gently roll up inside the kitchen towel, starting from one of the shorter ends. Don't roll too tightly or it will crack. Let cool while preparing the filling.
10. Vanilla Cream Filling:
11. In a small bowl, beat the cream cheese with 1/4 cup whipping cream until smooth.
12. In a large bowl, beat the remaining whipping cream with the sweetener and vanilla extract until it holds soft peaks. Then add the cream cheese mixture and continue to beat until stiff peaks form. Do not over-beat. Remove 1/2 cup and set aside for decorating.
13. Gently and carefully unroll the cake. Do not try to lay it completely flat, let it curl up on the ends. Spread with the remaining filling to within 1/2 inch of the edges. Gently roll back up without the kitchen towel. Place seam side-down on a serving platter.
14. Sprinkle with some more powdered sweetener, if desired. Pipe remaining vanilla cream mixture in stars or other shapes down the center of the top of the cake.
15. Refrigerate 1 hour before slicing. Store in the refrigerator.

Nutritional Facts:

- Calories: 206
- Fats: 18g
- Carbohydrates: 4g
- Proteins: 5g

Pumpkin Pie Cupcakes

Serves: 6

Cook Time: 30 minutes

Ingredients

- 3 tbsp coconut flour
- 1 tsp pumpkin pie spice
- 1/4 tsp baking powder
- 1/4 tsp baking soda
- Pinch salt
- 3/4 cup pumpkin puree
- 1/3 cup Swerve Brown or Swerve Granular
- 1/4 cup heavy whipping cream
- 1 large egg
- 1/2 tsp vanilla

Directions

1. Preheat oven to 350F and line 6 muffin cups with silicone or parchment liners.

2. In a small bowl, whisk together the coconut flour, pumpkin pie spice, baking powder, baking soda, and salt.
3. In a large bowl, whisk pumpkin puree, sweetener, cream, egg, and vanilla until well combined. Whisk in dry ingredients. If your batter seems very thin, whisk in an additional tbsp of coconut flour.
4. Divide among prepared muffin cups and bake 25 to 30 minutes, until just puffed and barely set. Remove from oven and let cool in pan (they will sink...that's okay, all the better for plopping your whipped cream on top!).
5. Refrigerate for at least one hour before serving. Dollop whipped cream generously on top.

Nutritional Facts:

- Calories: 70
- Fats: 4g
- Carbohydrates: 5g
- Proteins: 2g

Peanut Butter Blossoms

Serves: 30

Cook Time: 20 minutes

Ingredients

- Cookies:
- 1 ½ cups peanut flour
- 1 cup almond flour
- 3 tbsp coconut flour
- 1 tsp baking powder
- 1/2 tsp salt

- 1 cup creamy peanut butter
- 3/4 cup butter softened
- 1 cup Swerve Sweetener
- 2 eggs
- 1 tsp vanilla
- 1/4 cup Swerve or granulated erythritol or xylitol for sprinkling optional.
- Chocolate "Kisses":
- 6 oz sugar free dark chocolate
- 2 tbsp butter

Directions

1. Preheat oven to 325F and line several large baking sheets with parchment paper.
2. In a medium bowl, whisk together peanut flour, almond flour, coconut flour, baking powder, and salt.
3. In a large bowl, beat together the peanut butter and butter until creamy. Beat in sweetener, and then beat in eggs and vanilla until well combined.
4. Beat in peanut flour mixture until dough comes together.
5. Form dough into 1 inch balls and place 2 inches apart on prepared baking sheets. Wrap the bottom of a glass in plastic wrap and press each ball into a flat round, about 1/3 inch thick.
6. Use your thumb to press an indentation into the center of each cookie.
7. Bake about 15 minutes, until puffed and just barely beginning to brown (if you put more than one cookie sheet in the oven at a time, keep an eye on the one on the lower rack to make sure it doesn't brown too quickly).
8. Remove from oven. If needed, re-form the well in the center by gently pressing with the end of a wooden spoon. Sprinkle with granulated erythritol or xylitol of desired.

9. Let cool on pan 5 to 10 minutes, and then transfer to a wire rack to cool completely. Repeat with remaining dough.
10. For the chocolate kisses, melt butter and chocolate together in a small saucepan over low heat. Let cool until thickened enough to "dollop" into the well in each cookie.
11. Let set 1 hour.

Nutritional Facts:

- Calories: 165
- Fats: 14g
- Carbohydrates: 5g
- Proteins: 5g

Oatmeal Chocolate Chip Cookies

Serves: 24

Cook Time: 20 minutes

Ingredients

- 1 cup flaked coconut
- 3/4 cup sliced almonds
- 1 cup almond flour
- 1 tbsp coconut flour
- 1 tsp baking powder
- 1 tsp cinnamon
- 1/2 tsp salt
- 1/2 cup butter softened

- 1/2 cup Swerve Sweetener
- 1 large egg room temperature
- 1/2 tsp vanilla
- 1/2 cup sugar-free chocolate chips

Directions

1. Preheat oven to 325F and line a large baking sheet with parchment or a silicone liner.
2. In the bowl of a food processor, combine the flaked coconut and sliced almonds. Process until mixture resembles oatmeal. Add almond flour, coconut flour, baking powder, cinnamon, and salt and pulse a few times to combine.
3. In a large bowl, beat butter with sweetener until creamy. Beat in egg and vanilla extract and then beat in coconut/almond mixture until well combined. Stir in chocolate chips by hand.
4. Form into balls a little over 1 inch in diameter and place 2 inches apart on prepared baking sheet. With the heel of your hand, press cookies down to about 1/2 inch thickness.
5. Bake 15 to 18 minutes, until golden brown around the edges and just barely firm to the touch. Remove and let cool on pan.

Nutritional Facts:

- Calories: 115
- Fats: 10g
- Carbohydrates: 5g
- Proteins: 3g

Chocolate Hazelnut Sandwich Cookies

Serves: 20

Cook Time: 20 minutes

Ingredients

- Cookies:
- 2 cups Hazelnut Meal
- 1 tsp baking powder
- 1/8 tsp salt
- 1/4 cup butter
- 1/4 cup hazelnut oil
- 1/2 cup granulated Swerve Sweetener
- 1 large egg
- 1/2 tsp vanilla extract
- Chocolate Ganache Filling:
- 3 & 1/2 tbsp butter
- 1 & 1/2 ounces good-quality unsweetened chocolate chopped
- 3 tbsp powdered Swerve Sweetener
- 1/4 tsp vanilla extract

Directions

1. Cookies:
2. Preheat oven to 325F and line a large baking sheet with parchment paper.
3. In a medium bowl, whisk together hazelnut meal, baking powder and salt.
4. In a large bowl, beat butter and hazelnut oil with granulated sweetener until well combined. Beat in egg and vanilla extract.
5. Beat in hazelnut meal mixture until dough comes together.

6. Roll dough into scant 1-inch balls and place 2 inches apart on prepared baking sheet (you should get about 36 balls). Press balls down to 1/4 inch thickness with the heel of your hand.
7. Bake 12 to 14 minutes, until just beginning to brown around the edges and just barely firm to the touch.
8. Remove and let cool on pan 10 minutes, then transfer to a wire rack to cool completely (they will continue to crisp up as they cool).
9. Chocolate Ganache Filling:
10. In a microwaveable safe bowl, combine butter and chopped chocolate. Heat in 20 second increments, stirring in between, until melted.
11. Stir in powdered sweetener and vanilla extract until smooth. Let sit about 10 minutes to thicken.
12. Spread about 1 tsp ganache on the bottom of one cookie and then top with another cookie, bottom-side in.
13. Repeat with remaining cookies and remaining ganache.

Nutritional Facts:

- Calories: 164
- Fats: 17g
- Carbohydrates: 3g
- Proteins: 3g

Cranberry Pecan Biscotti

Serves: 15

Prep Time: 55 minutes

Ingredients

- Biscotti:
- 2 cups almond flour
- ½ cup granular Swerve Sweetener
- 1 tsp baking powder
- ½ tsp xanthan gum (can also sub 1 tbsp coconut flour)
- 1 tbsp orange zest
- ¼ cup butter melted
- 1 large egg lightly beaten
- ½ tsp vanilla extract
- 1/4 cup chopped pecans
- 1/4 cup sugar-free dried cranberries
- Chocolate Dip:
- 3 ounces sugar-free dark chocolate chopped
- 1/2 ounce cocoa butter (or 1 tbsp coconut oil)

Directions

1. Biscotti:
2. Preheat oven to 325F and line a baking sheet with parchment paper.
3. In a large bowl, whisk together almond flour, Swerve, baking powder and xanthan gum. Stir in orange zest.
4. Stir together melted butter, egg, and vanilla extract until dough comes together. Add pecans and dried cranberries and stir until mixed throughout.
5. Turn dough out onto baking sheet and form into low, flat log, 10 x 4 inches. Bake 25 minutes, or until lightly browned and firm to the

touch. Remove from oven and let cool 30 minutes. Reduce oven temperature to 250F.
6. With a sharp knife, gently cut into 15 even slices. Place slices back onto baking sheet cut-side down and bake for 15 minutes, then flip each slice and continue to bake for another 15 minutes. Turn off oven and let sit inside until cool.
7. Chocolate Dip:
8. In microwave or double boiler, melt chocolate until smooth. Dip ends of biscotti in and lay on a waxed paper lined baking sheet until set (you can chill them to set the chocolate faster).

Nutritional Facts:

- Calories: 242
- Fats: 23g
- Carbohydrates: 6g
- Proteins: 4g

5. SEASONING

Blackened Seasoning

Serves: 1

Prep Time: 5 minutes

Ingredients

- 1 tablespoon plus 1 1/2 teaspoons smoked paprika
- 1 tablespoon garlic powder
- 1 tablespoon onion powder
- 1 tablespoon dried thyme leaves
- 1 teaspoon cayenne pepper
- 1 teaspoon dried basil
- 1 teaspoon cumin
- 1 teaspoon celery salt
- 1/2 teaspoon dried oregano

Directions

1. Combine all spices and store in an air tight spice jar or mason jar. I like to use mason jars and these lids.

Nutritional Facts:

- Calories: 96
- Fats: 3g
- Carbohydrates: 12g
- Proteins: 4g

Jamaican Jerk Seasoning

Serves: 1

Prep Time: 5 minutes

Ingredients

- 1 tablespoon onion flakes
- 2 teaspoons ground thyme
- 1 teaspoon dried parsley
- 1 teaspoon ground allspice
- ¼ teaspoon ground cinnamon
- 1 teaspoon ground black pepper
- ½ teaspoon cayenne pepper
- 1 teaspoon paprika
- ½ teaspoon hot pepper flakes
- ¼ teaspoon ground cumin
- 1 tablespoon garlic powder
- 2 teaspoons salt
- ¼ teaspoon ground nutmeg
- 2 teaspoons sugar
- 2 teaspoons dried jalapenos

Directions

1. Mix together all ingredients.
2. Store leftovers in a tightly closed glass jar.

Nutritional Facts:

- Calories: 96
- Fats: 3g
- Carbohydrates: 12g
- Proteins: 4g

Cajun Seasoning

Serves: 5

Prep Time: 2 minutes

Ingredients

- 1 tbsp ground cumin
- 1 tbsp ground coriander
- 1 tbsp paprika
- 3/4 tsp salt
- 3/4 tsp cracked pepper
- 3/4 tsp oregano
- 3/4 tsp basil
- 3/4 tsp thyme
- 1 1/2 tsp white pepper
- 1 1/2 tsp cayenne pepper if you want the heat

Directions

1. Combine all the spices together and keep in an airtight container.

Nutritional Facts:

- Calories: 21
- Fats: 1g
- Carbohydrates: 3g
- Proteins: 1g

Gingerbread Spice Mix

Serves: 8

Prep Time: 5 minutes

Ingredients

- 2 tbsp ground cinnamon
- 2 tbsp ground ginger
- 2 tbsp ground allspice
- 1 tbsp ground nutmeg
- 1/2 tbsp ground cloves
- Pinch ground black pepper

Directions

1. Mix all the spices in a small bowl.
2. Seal in an airtight jar. (I like small Mason jars for this job.)

Nutritional Facts:

- Calories: 18
- Fats: 0g
- Carbohydrates: 4g
- Proteins: 0g

Montreal Steak Seasoning

Serves: 5

Prep Time: 5 minutes

Ingredients

- 4 tablespoons salt
- 1 tablespoon black pepper
- 1 tablespoon dehydrated onion
- 1/2 tablespoon dehydrated garlic
- 1/2 tablespoon crushed red pepper
- 1/2 tablespoon dried thyme
- 1/2 tablespoon dried rosemary
- 1/2 tablespoon dried fennel

Directions

1. Mix together and store in a shaker. Shake or rub 1 tablespoon seasoning onto 1 pound steaks, pork chops and hamburgers before grilling or broiling.

Nutritional Facts:

- Calories: 18
- Fats: 0g
- Carbohydrates: 4g
- Proteins: 0g

BBQ Seasoning

Serves: 4

Prep Time: 5 minutes

Ingredients

- 3 tsp smoked paprika
- 1 tsp sea salt

- 1 tsp black pepper
- 1/2 tsp ground mustard
- 1/2 tsp garlic powder
- 1/2 tsp ground sage
- 1/2 tsp cinnamon
- 1/4 tsp allspice
- 1/4 tsp nutmeg

Directions

1. Mix all ingredients in a small bowl. Store in an airtight container until usage.

Nutritional Facts:

- Calories: 8
- Fats: 0g
- Carbohydrates: 1g
- Proteins: 0g

Lemon Pepper Seasoning

Serves: 1

Prep Time: 5 minutes

Ingredients

- 5+ large lemons
- 1/3 cup {scant} of crushed pepper corns {black and/or medley}
- 1/4 cup kosher salt

Directions

1. Zest all the lemons and mix with crushed peppercorns.
2. Spread out on parchment lined baking sheet and bake on lowest setting until the zest is completely dried.
3. Add the lemon-pepper to a spice grinder and grind until desired texture.
4. Mix with the kosher salt if desired and store in a airtight container for up to a few months.

Nutritional Facts:

- Calories: 28
- Fats: 0g
- Carbohydrates: 3g
- Proteins: 0g

Pumpkin Pie Spice

Serves: 1

Prep Time: 5 minutes

Ingredients

- ¼ cup cinnamon
- 2 tablespoons ground ginger
- 1 tablespoon ground nutmeg
- 2 teaspoons ground cloves

Directions

1. Combine all ingredients and store in an airtight container or spice jar.

Nutritional Facts:

- Calories: 28
- Fats: 0g
- Carbohydrates: 3g
- Proteins: 0g

Taco Seasoning

Serves: 1

Prep Time: 5 minutes

Ingredients

- 2 tablespoons chili powder
- 2 tablespoons cumin
- 2 teaspoons onion powder
- 2 teaspoons garlic powder
- 2 teaspoons celery salt
- ½ teaspoon cayenne pepper
- ½ teaspoon black pepper
- ½ teaspoon sea salt

Directions

1. Combine all ingredients in an airtight spice jar.

Nutritional Facts:

- Calories: 151
- Fats: 5g
- Carbohydrates: 15g
- Proteins: 7g

Dry Ranch Seasoning

Serves: 1

Prep Time: 5 minutes

Ingredients

- 1/3 cup dry powdered buttermilk
- 2 tablespoons dried parsley
- 1 1/2 teaspoons dried dill weed
- 2 teaspoons garlic powder
- 2 teaspoons onion powder
- 2 teaspoons dried onion flakes
- 1 teaspoon ground black pepper
- 1 teaspoon dried chives
- 1 teaspoon salt

Directions

1. Whisk all ingredients together until blended. If you want a more finely-ground seasoning mix, you can pulse the mixture in a food processor until it reaches your desired consistency.

2. Store in a sealed container (here is the jar I used) in the refrigerator for up to 3 months.

Nutritional Facts:

- Calories: 151
- Fats: 5g
- Carbohydrates: 15g
- Proteins: 7g

Poultry Seasoning

Serves: 1

Prep Time: 5 minutes

Ingredients

- 1 tbsp dried thyme
- 1 tbsp sage
- 1 tbsp dried onion flakes
- 1 ½ tsp sea salt
- 1 ½ tsp garlic powder
- ¾ tsp black pepper

Directions

1. Combine all spices and store in an air tight container or glass spice jar.

Nutritional Facts:

- Calories: 50
- Fats: 0g

- Carbohydrates: 9g
- Proteins: 2g

Dry Onion Soup Mix

Serves: 1

Prep Time: 5 minutes

Ingredients

- 4 tbsp dried onion flakes
- 2 tbsp powdered beef bouillon
- 1 tsp onion powder
- 1 tsp garlic powder
- 1 tsp dried parsley
- ¼ tsp celery salt
- ¼ tsp black pepper

Directions

1. Combine all ingredients and store in an air tight spice jar when not in use.

Nutritional Facts:

- Calories: 110
- Fats: 0g
- Carbohydrates: 23g
- Proteins: 2g

6. MEAT

Cabbage Beef Skillet

Serves: 4

Cook Time: 15 minutes

Ingredients

- 1/2 head green cabbage, sliced in shreds
- 2 tablespoons butter, unsalted
- 1 pound ground beef
- 3 tablespoons Taco Seasoning Mix
- 1 teaspoon dried minced onion
- 1 1/2 cups Mexican Cheese Blend
- salt and pepper to taste

Directions

1. Preheat oven to 350 degrees.
2. In a large skillet add 1 tablespoon of butter and saute cabbage on medium high heat until the cabbage softens. Remove from heat and place cabbage in a separate dish.
3. In the same skillet add the remaining tablespoon of butter and cook ground beef breaking up meat as it cooks. Add taco seasoning, onion and stir until meat is cooked. If the meat is dry add up to 1/4 cup of water. Return cabbage to skillet and season with salt and pepper. Fold in 1/2 cup of cheese. Top skillet with remaining cheese and place in the oven. Cook until cheese melts (10 minutes).

Nutritional Facts:

- Calories: 302
- Fats: 22g
- Carbohydrates: 10g
- Proteins: 24g

Beef Stroganoff Meatballs

Serves: 4

Cook Time: 30 minutes

Ingredients

- For the meatball mix:
- 1 lb ground beef (80/20)
- 1 egg
- 1/4 cup almond flour
- 1 tsp kosher salt
- 1/4 tsp black pepper
- 1/2 tsp garlic powder
- 1/2 tsp onion powder
- 1 tsp dried parsley
- 1 tsp Worcestershire sauce
- 2 Tbsp butter (for frying)
- For the sauce:
- 1 Tbsp butter
- 2 cups sliced mushrooms (white or cremini)
- 1 cup sliced onions
- 1 clove garlic, minced
- 1 1/2 cups beef broth
- 3/4 cup sour cream
- 1/4 tsp xanthan gum

- salt and pepper to taste
- 2 Tbsp fresh parsley, chopped

Directions

1. Combine the meatball ingredients (except the butter) in a medium bowl and mix well.
2. Form into 12 meatballs.
3. Heat the 2 Tbsp of butter in a large, nonstick saute pan.
4. Cook the meatballs on medium heat in the butter until browned on all sides and cooked through (2-3 minutes per side.)
5. Remove the meatballs from the pan and set aside.
6. Add the 1 Tbsp of butter and the 2 cups of sliced mushrooms to the pan.
7. Cook until the mushrooms are golden and fragrant (4-5 minutes.)
8. Remove the mushrooms from the pan.
9. Add the onions and garlic and cook for 3-4 minutes or until softened and translucent.
10. Remove the onions from the pan.
11. Add the beef broth to your pan and scrape the bottom to get all the yummy bits off.
12. Whisk in your sour cream and xanthan gum until smooth.
13. Add the meatballs, mushrooms, onions and garlic back to the pan and stir.
14. Simmer on low for 20 minutes.
15. Season with salt and pepper to taste.
16. Garnish with the fresh parsley right before serving.

Nutritional Facts:

- Calories: 452
- Fats: 34g
- Carbohydrates: 6g
- Proteins: 24g

Crockpot Beef Stew

Serves: 9

Cook Time: 6 Hours

Ingredients

- 1 1/4 lb Beef Stew Meat
- 2 tablespoons olive oil
- 1 tablespoon butter
- 1/2 medium onion
- 3 garlic cloves minced
- 8 oz mushrooms sliced
- 1 tablespoon parsley
- 1 teaspoon rosemary
- 1 teaspoon paprika
- 1 teaspoon salt
- 1 teaspoon pepper
- 1/2 teaspoon thyme
- 2 tablespoons tomato paste
- 2 tablespoons Worcestershire sauce
- 2 tablespoons Bragg Liquid Aminos
- 1/2 lb radishes cut into cubes
- 1 celery rib chopped
- 1 can green beans drained
- 1/2 of a 14oz can Italian diced tomatoes
- 4 cups beef broth
- 2 bay leaves
- 1 tsp Xanthan Gum

Directions

1. Brown Beef Stew in a skillet over medium-high heat in olive oil and butter. It is best to brown in two batches so that the skillet remains hot and quickly sears the meat.
2. Once it has browned on all sides, add to crock-pot.
3. In the same skillet, add onions, garlic, mushrooms, and all the spices except the bay leaves and saute for 3-4 minutes.
4. Add the sauteed veggies and the rest of the ingredients to the crock-pot except the Xanthan Gum.
5. Cook on high 6-7 hours or low for 10 hours.
6. Thirty minutes before serving, remove the lid, sprinkle Xanthan Gum on top, and stir.
7. Leave the lid off and allow Beef Stew to simmer and thicken for approx 30 minutes.
8. Serve.

Nutritional Facts:

- Calories: 185
- Fats: 9g
- Carbohydrates: 4g
- Proteins: 20g

Unstuffed Cabbage Soup

Serves: 9

Cook Time: 45 minutes

Ingredients

- 1/2 of a small onion diced

- 2 garlic cloves minced
- 1 1/2 lbs 80/20 ground beef
- 3 cups beef broth
- 1 14 oz can diced tomatoes
- 1 8 oz can tomato sauce
- 1/4 cup Bragg's Aminos
- 1 small/medium cabbage chopped
- 3 tsp Worcestershire Sauce
- 1/2 tsp parsley
- 1/2 tsp salt
- 1/2 tsp pepper

Directions

1. In a stock pot brown ground beef with onions and garlic.
2. Drain then return to pot.
3. Add all other ingredients and cook covered on low/medium for 45 min to 1 hour or until cabbage is tender.

Nutritional Facts:

- Calories: 117
- Fats: 14g
- Carbohydrates: 6g
- Proteins: 15g

Beef Taquitos

Serves: 6

Cook Time: 12 minutes

Ingredients

- 1 Cup Shredded Cheddar Cheese
- 1 Cup Shredded Mozzarella Cheese
- ½ Cup Grated Parmesan Cheese
- ½ lb Ground Beef
- ¼ Cup Minced Onion
- 1 Tsp Cumin
- ½ Tsp Chili Powder
- ½ Tsp Paprika
- ½ Tsp Onion Powder
- ½ Tsp Garlic Power
- ½ Tsp Salt
- ½ Tsp Pepper
- ½ Cup Water

Directions

1. Brown the beef with the minced onion. In a cup mix the cumin, chilli powder, onion and garlic powder and salt and pepper with the water. Then pour over the browned ground beef. Let simmer for 5 - 10 minutes or until all the liquid is evaporated.
2. In a large mixing bowl, mix the cheddar, mozzarella and parmesan cheeses. Divide the cheese mixture into 6 then make balls. Place onto a parchment paper lined baking sheet. Bake @ 400 F for 6-8 minutes, or until the edges are golden brown.
3. Let cool for 1- 2 minutes. Flip upside down, then place a few spoonfuls of the beef on the edge of each shell. Tightly roll each

one into a cigar shape. (You need to do this quite quickly, before the cheese hardens)
4. This recipe makes 6 Keto Beef Taquitos.
5. Note: To reheat, Preheat oven to 350 F. Bake for 6-8 minutes.

Nutritional Facts:

- Calories: 231
- Fats: 17g
- Carbohydrates: 2g
- Proteins: 16g

Italian Meatball Casserole

Serves: 6

Cook Time: 2 hours

Ingredients

- 1¼ lb Ground Beef 80/20
- ½ cup grated parmesan cheese
- ½ cup mozzarella cheese
- 2 tablespoons coconut flour
- 2 eggs
- ¾ tsp salt
- ¾ tsp minced onion
- ¼ tsp Italian seasoning
- 1/2 tsp garlic powder
- ¼ tsp black pepper
- 24 oz jar low carb spaghetti sauce
- 2 cups mozzarella cheese

- 1 teaspoon basil to sprinkle on top of cheeses

Directions

1. Combine all ingredients except the last three ingredients in a bowl and stir to combine.
2. Heat a cast iron skillet on medium on the stove.
3. Cover the bottom of the skillet with ¼ inch coconut oil.
4. When the oil gets hot, scoop meatballs with a cookie scoop into hot oil and brown.
5. Once the meatballs are browned, place in the bottom of a crock pot.
6. Pour spaghetti sauce on top of the meatballs.
7. Cook on high for 2-3 hours or low 4-5.
8. Scoop out meatballs into a casserole dish.
9. Sprinkle mozzarella cheese then basil on top.
10. Broil in the oven on the top rack for 2-3 minutes or until the cheese starts to bubble and brown.

Nutritional Facts:

- Calories: 485
- Fats: 34g
- Carbohydrates: 5g
- Proteins: 36g

Mongolian Beef

Serves: 4

Cook Time: 10 minutes

Ingredients

- 1 lb Flat Iron steak , thinly sliced against the grain
- 1/4 cup Coconut Oil
- 3 Green onions , cut into 1-inch long diagonal slices
- Low Carb Mongolian Beef Marinade
- 1/4 cup Coconut Aminos
- 1 teaspoon Ginger , grated
- 2 cloves Garlic , chopped

Directions

1. Cut the Flat Iron Steak into very thin slices against the grain.
2. Add the sliced beef to a small ziplock bag and add the coconut aminos, ginger, and garlic. Let marinate for 1 hour in the fridge.
3. When you are ready to cook, drain the meat from the marinade but reserve the liquid for later.
4. Add the coconut oil to a large wok or cast iron skillet and heat it until it's almost smoking, the oil must be hot so you can get the nice crispy edges on the beef.
5. Add the beef to the very hot oil (you may need to do it in two batches, don't crowd the pan) and keep stir frying over a high heat, taking care not to burn it for just 1-3 minutes.
6. When the last batch of meat is in, add the green onions and cook for the last 30 seconds to 1 minute.
7. If you want more 'sauce' to serve with the meat quickly cook the remaining marinade for just a minute or two in your wok after the last batch of beef has been cooked, and serve with the beef.
8. Serve immediately!

Nutritional Facts:

- Calories: 337
- Fats: 25g
- Carbohydrates: 4g
- Proteins: 21g

Italian Pork & Parmesan Meatballs

Serves: 4

Cook Time: 20 minutes

Ingredients

- For the meatballs:
- 1 lb ground pork
- 1/3 cup almond flour
- 2 Tbsp water
- 1/4 cup grated parmesan cheese
- 1/4 cup parsley, finely chopped
- 1 egg
- 1/2 tsp garlic powder
- 1/2 tsp kosher salt
- 1/4 tsp ground black pepper
- 2 Tbsp olive oil
- For the greens:
- 1 Tbsp olive oil
- 1 garlic clove, thinly sliced
- 4 cups fresh arugula, packed (or spinach or swiss chard)
- For the Sauce:
- 1 Tbsp olive oil

- 1/4 cup onion, chopped
- 1 clove garlic, minced
- 1 cup crushed tomatoes
- 1 cup chicken broth
- 1/2 tsp lemon zest
- 2 Tbsp heavy whipping cream
- 1 tsp fresh oregano, chopped
- For the cauliflower puree:
- 5 cups cauliflower florets
- 2 Tbsp heavy whipping cream
- 2 Tbsp butter
- 1/4 cup freshly grated parmesan cheese
- salt and pepper to taste

Directions

1. To make the meatballs:
2. Combine all of the meatball ingredients (except for the olive oil) in a medium bowl and mix thoroughly.
3. Form into 15 meatballs.
4. Heat the olive oil in a non-stick saute pan, then cook the meatballs in small batches, turning occasionally until golden brown and cooked through. Set aside.
5. To make the greens:
6. In a medium saute pan, heat the olive oil and garlic.
7. Cook for a minute or two until the garlic is fragrant and sizzling.
8. Add the arugula (or other greens) and cook for a minute or two, until just wilted and still bright green. Remove from the pan and set aside.
9. To make the sauce:
10. Add the olive oil, onion, and garlic to the same pan you cooked the greens in and cook for a couple of minutes until the onions are translucent but not browned.

11. Add the tomatoes and chicken broth and simmer for about 10 minutes.
12. Stir in the lemon zest, heavy whipping cream, and fresh oregano.
13. Cook for 2 – 3 minutes and remove from the heat.
14. To make the cauliflower puree:
15. Combine the cauliflower, butter, and heavy cream in a microwave safe bowl.
16. Microwave, uncovered, on high for 10 minutes.
17. Stir to coat cauliflower with cream/butter mixture.
18. Microwave for another 6-8 minutes on high or until completely soft.
19. Remove from the microwave and put into a high speed blender or food processor along with the cheese.
20. Puree until smooth.
21. Season with salt and pepper to taste. You can adjust the cream and butter to your preference.
22. To assemble:
23. Spread 1/2 cup cauliflower puree on your serving plate.
24. Top with 3 meatballs.
25. Add about 1/4 cup of the wilted greens around the meatballs.
26. Spoon about 1/3 cup of sauce over the top.
27. Garnish with additional lemon zest, oregano, and grated parmesan cheese if desired.

Nutritional Facts:

- Calories: 535
- Fats: 40g
- Carbohydrates: 7g
- Proteins: 23g

Pork Egg Roll In A Bowl

Serves: 4

Cook Time: 25 minutes

Ingredients

- 2 tablespoons sesame oil
- 3 cloves garlic, minced
- 1/2 cup onion, diced
- 5 green onions, sliced on a bias (white and green parts)
- 1 pound ground pork
- 1/2 teaspoon ground ginger
- sea salt and black pepper, to taste
- 1 tablespoon Sriracha or garlic chili sauce, more to taste (omit or use a compliant brand for Whole30)
- 14 ounce bag coleslaw mix
- 3 tablespoons Coconut Aminos or gluten free soy sauce
- 1 tablespoon rice vinegar
- 2 tablespoons toasted sesame seeds

Directions

1. Heat sesame oil in a large skillet over medium high heat.
2. Add the garlic, onion, and white portion of the green onions. Sauté until the onions are translucent and the garlic is fragrant.
3. Add the ground pork, ground ginger, sea salt, black pepper and Sriracha. Sauté until the pork is cooked through.
4. Add the coleslaw mix, coconut aminos, and rice wine vinegar. Sauté until the coleslaw is tender.
5. Top with green onions and sesame seeds before serving.

Nutritional Facts:

- Calories: 297
- Fats: 20g
- Carbohydrates: 7g
- Proteins: 20g

Bacon Covered Meatloaf

Serves: 12

Cook Time: 20 minutes

Ingredients

- 1 spring onion sliced
- 2 cloves garlic crushed
- 750 g mince/ground beef
- 750 g mince/ground pork
- 2 eggs - medium lightly beaten
- handful fresh parsley chopped
- handful fresh basil chopped
- 2 slices bacon diced
- 2 tbsp sun-dried tomatoes chopped
- 2 tsp dried oregano
- salt and pepper to taste
- vegetables of choice diced/grated/shredded
- 6 slices bacon to cover the meatloaf
- Optional - if not paleo you can add 100g / 3.5 grated cheese of choice to the meatloaf mixture

Directions

1. Oil and line a baking tray before starting.
2. Put all the ingredients in a large mixing bowl and mix together with your hands until all the ingredients are thoroughly incorporated together.
3. Form into a large meatloaf shape on the lined baking tray. Cover with the bacon slices and sprinkle on parmesan cheese (optional).
4. Bake at 180C/350F for 50 minutes or until thoroughly cooked in the centre.

Nutritional Facts:

- Calories: 370
- Fats: 25g
- Carbohydrates: 2g
- Proteins: 35g

Ground Pork Tacos

Serves: 1

Cook Time: 15 minutes

Ingredients

- 400 grams of ground pork (about 13 oz.)
- 1/2 tsp
- garlic powder
- 1/2 tsp
- onion powder
- 1/2 tsp sea salt
- 1/8 tsp
- cumin
- 1/8 tsp ground pepper

- 5 tbsp salsa
- 5 or more lettuce leaves (I used Boston Red Leaf Lettuce)
- taco toppings like diced green peppers/red peppers/avocado/onions etc.

Directions

1. In a small bowl, mix using your hands, the ground pork and all the seasoning (except the salsa).
2. Place the meat in a frying pan and turn the heat to medium. Constantly stir the meat making sure to breakup any large pieces.
3. Once the meat is cooked drain the fat from the pan.
4. Add the salsa and mix.
5. Place the meat on the lettuce wraps and top with your favourite taco toppings.

Nutritional Facts:

- Calories: 370
- Fats: 25g
- Carbohydrates: 2g
- Proteins: 35g

Spinach And Italian Sausage Stuffed Pork Tenderloin

Serves: 6

Cook Time: 50 minutes

Ingredients

- 1-2 tbsp ghee
- 1 large onion, chopped

- 454g (1lb) spinach, chopped
- ¼ tsp Himalayan salt
- ¼ tsp freshly cracked black pepper
- ½lb mushrooms, chopped
- 2 -454g (1lb) pork tenderloins
- 3 spicy Italian sausages, removed from casing
- 10-12 slices pasture raised bacon

Directions

1. Preheat oven to 375F
2. Melt 1 tablespoon of ghee in a large skillet set over medium heat. Add onion, salt and pepper and cook until the onion turns translucent, about 3-5 minutes.
3. Add chopped spinach and cook until just wilted. Transfer the cooked spinach to a fine mesh sieve and set it to cool for a few minutes.
4. Meanwhile, return your skillet to the heat source and melt the remaining tablespoon of ghee. Add the mushrooms and cook until softened and golden, about 2 minutes. Remove from heat and set aside to cool.
5. Squeeze as much water as you possibly can out of the spinach by pushing it down in the sieve with a small plate or the back of a ladle. Set aside.
6. Now slice your tenderloins open. To do that, place the blade of your knife parallel to your cutting board, put your hand flat on top of the tenderloin and carefully slice down the middle almost all the way to the end. You'll want to stop about ¾ of the way through.
7. Lay the tenderloins open on a cutting board and, with a meat mallet or small saucepan, delicately pound them until they're about ½ inch thick.
8. Place your now flat tenderloins on your cutting board, sprinkle with salt and pepper, then divide and spread the sausage meat on both tenderloins, as evenly as possible but without going all the

way to the edge; you want to leave about one inch all around. Top with spinach mixture, followed with mushrooms.
9. Roll the tenderloins as tightly as you can, taking care to place the seam underneath, then carefully wrap each of them with the bacon strips by simply going around. You should need 5 or 6 strips per tenderloin.
10. Transfer your wrapped pork to an oven safe baking dish, cover with aluminum foil and bake in a 375F oven for 35-40 minutes.
11. Remove foil and continue cooking for 20-25 minutes, basting 2-3 times during that period.
12. Set your oven to broil and finish crisping up the bacon, which should take anywhere from 3 to 5 minutes. Keep a close eye on the prize, during that time: you wouldn't want your precious bundles to burn!
13. Remove from oven, tent loosely and let the meat rest for 10-15 minutes before slicing.

Nutritional Facts:

- Calories: 306
- Fats: 15g
- Carbohydrates: 7g
- Proteins: 36g

Apple Dijon Pork Chops

Serves: 2

Cook Time: 10 minutes

Ingredients

- 2 pork chops (320 g)

- 4 Tablespoons of ghee (60 ml)
- 2 Tablespoons of applesauce (30 ml)
- 2 Tablespoons of ghee (30 ml)
- 2 Tablespoons of Dijon mustard (30 ml)
- Salt and pepper, to taste

Directions

1. Melt the 4 Tablespoons of ghee in a large pan.
2. Add in the pork chops. Using tongs, position the pork chops on its side so that the fat cooks in the ghee first. This makes browns and renders the fat a bit. Then once the fat is a bit crispy and browned, lay the pork chops flat in the ghee.
3. Cook for 3-4 minutes on each side. Check using a meat thermometer that the internal temperature of the pork reaches 145 F (63 C). When you cut into the pork chops, you'll find it has a medium rare pink inside. If you prefer your pork chops more cooked, then just leave it in there for longer.
4. Meanwhile, mix the applesauce, melted ghee, and mustard together well.
5. Serve the pork chops with the sauce and season with salt and pepper to taste.

Nutritional Facts:

- Calories: 560
- Fats: 50g
- Carbohydrates: 2g
- Proteins: 36g

7. FISH

Salmon With Creamy Dill Sauce

Serves: 4

Cook Time: 5 minutes

Ingredients

- DILL SAUCE
- 3/4 cup sour cream
- 2 tsp Dijon or hot English mustard
- 1/2 tsp garlic powder or 1 small garlic clove, minced
- 2 1/2 tbsp fresh dill, finely chopped
- 1 tsp lemon zest
- 1 - 2 tbsp lemon juice
- 2 tbsp milk (or olive oil, for richness)
- 1/4 - 1/2 tsp salt
- 1/2 tsp white sugar
- FISH
- 1/2 - 1 tbsp oil
- 4 salmon or trout fillets (125g / 4oz each)
- Salt and pepper

Directions

1. Mix the Dill Sauce ingredients together (Mix well to loosen the sour cream). Adjust consistency with milk and tartness with lemon juice. Set aside for 10 minutes if you can - if using fresh garlic, set aside for 20 min.
2. Pat fish dry with paper towel. Sprinkle with salt and pepper.

3. Heat oil in skillet over medium high heat. Place fish in skillet skin side down. Cook for 2 minutes, then flip and cook the other side for 1 1/2 minutes.
4. Remove from skillet onto serving plates. Serve with Dill Sauce on the side, garnished with fresh dill and lemon wedges if desired.

Nutritional Facts:

- Calories: 397
- Fats: 22g
- Carbohydrates: 7g
- Proteins: 44g

Salmon With Bacon & Tomato Cream Sauce

Serves: 2

Cook Time: 15 minutes

Ingredients

- Fishpeople Seafood Salmon
- 2-6 ounce filets Sockeye or Keta salmon
- Bacon Tomato Vodka Cream Sauce
- 2 slices bacon, diced
- 1 teaspoons of bacon grease or olive oil
- 1 clove garlic, sliced
- 1 ounce onion, sliced (about 1/4 of a medium onion)
- 1/4 cup vodka (2 oz/ 60 ml)
- 1 tablespoon tomato paste (15 g)
- 1/3 cup heavy cream (2 1/2 oz/ 75 ml)
- 2 tablespoons water (1 oz/ 30 ml0

- 1 tablespoon vodka (1/2 oz/ 15 ml)
- 10 leaves basil, chiffonade
- 1/2 teaspoon lemon zest, grated
- salt and pepper to taste

Directions

1. Preparation: Let the Salmon come to temperature on the counter for 15 minutes. Gather all of the ingredients. Dice the bacon.
2. Bacon: Place a medium-sized frying pan over medium heat. Add the bacon and 1 teaspoon of bacon grease and stir, coating the bacon. Let cook about 2 minutes. Meanwhile, slice the onion and garlic, chiffonade the basil, and grate the lemon zest. (To chiffonade, stack the basil leaves, roll them lengthwise then cutting crosswise, slice into thin ribbons.) Give the bacon in the pan a stir and cook until browned and crisp. Remove the bacon leaving the fat in the pan.
3. Salmon: Pour out all of the bacon fat from the frying pan except about 2 tablespoons and return pan to the stove over medium heat. Very lightly salt each salmon filet and lay them in the pan, pretty-side down (or skin-side up - I removed the skin on my pieces). Let cook undisturbed for about 3-4 minutes depending on thickness. You'll see the salmon become lighter where it has cooked, this will let you judge if it's time to flip. (You'll want that color change almost half-way before flipping.) Flip the fish with a spatula and cook again for approximately 3-4 minutes. Remove the salmon to a plate and tent gently with a piece of foil to keep warm.
4. Sauce: Return the pan to the stove, keeping the heat set to just below medium. Add the onions and garlic and stir until they begin to soften - about 1 1/2 minutes. Move the pan off of the burner, and while STANDING BACK,slowly add the vodka. Return the pan to the heat stirring to lift up the browned bits from the bottom of the pan. Let the vodka reduce by half.

5. Add the tomato paste and stir it around the onions to warm it up and help break it down. Add the heavy cream and water, stirring to combine. Let it simmer gently for a minute to thicken up a little. Add the bacon, 1 tablespoon of vodka, and lemon zest. Stir the sauce until the sharp smell of alcohol has dissipated. Add the basil. Taste and add a pinch of salt and pepper to your taste. Turn off the heat.
6. Plate: Place a salmon filet on a serving plate and top with half of the sauce. Garnish with more basil if desired.

Nutritional Facts:

- Calories: 431
- Fats: 19g
- Carbohydrates: 6g
- Proteins: 38g

Avocado & Basil Salmon

Serves: 4

Cook Time: 10 minutes

Ingredients

- 2 teaspoons coconut oil
- 1 ½ teaspoon coarse kosher salt, divided
- 1 teaspoon Italian seasonings
- ½ teaspoon crushed red pepper
- ¼ teaspoon ground black pepper

- 1 ½ pounds boneless salmon filet, skin removed
- 1 avocado
- ¼ cup chopped basil
- 1 tablespoon lime juice
- chopped scallions, for garnish

Directions

1. Heat oil in a large cast iron skillet over medium high heat. Sprinkle ¾ teaspoon salt, Italian seasonings, crushed red pepper and black pepper all over the salmon. Lay salmon filet skinned side up in the hot oil. Let cook, undisturbed until browned and crispy along the bottom edge, and the flesh is opaque about half way up the side of the filet, 4 to 6 minutes, depending on thickness.
2. Flip salmon over and remove skillet from heat. Allow salmon to remain in hot skillet to allow the carry-over heat to continue cooking the other side to desired doneness, about 4 minutes more.
3. Meanwhile, peel pit and mash avocado with basil, lime juice and the remaining ¾ teaspoon salt.
4. Serve salmon topped with avocado mash sprinkled with scallions if desired.

Nutritional Facts:

- Calories: 323
- Fats: 9g
- Carbohydrates: 6g
- Proteins: 32g

Salmon & Asparagus Foil Packs

Serves: 4

Cook Time: 20 minutes

Ingredients

- 4 (6 oz) skinless salmon fillets
- 1 lb asparagus , tough ends trimmed
- 2 1/2 Tbsp olive oil
- 2 cloves garlic , minced
- Salt and freshly ground black pepper
- 1 lemon thinly sliced
- Fresh dill sprigs , or chopped fresh thyme, rosemary or parsley

Directions

1. Preheat oven to 400 degrees. Cut four sheets of aluminum foil about 14-inch long. Divide asparagus into 4 equal portions (about 8 spears per foil packet) and layer in center of each length of foil.
2. In a small bowl stir together oil with garlic. Drizzle 1 tsp of the oil over portion of asparagus then sprinkle with salt and pepper. Rinse salmon and allow excess water to run off, then season bottom of each fillet with salt and pepper. Layer fillets over asparagus.
3. Drizzle top of each salmon fillet with 1 tsp of the olive oil mixture and season top with salt and pepper to taste. Top each with about 2 sprigs dill and 2 lemon slices (if using fresh thyme or rosemary use about 3/4 tsp per each if using parsley use 1 1/2 tsp).
4. Wrap sides of foil inward over salmon then fold in top and bottom of foil to enclose.
5. Place foil pouches in a single layer on a baking sheet. Bake in preheated oven until salmon is cooked through, about 25 - 30 minutes. Unwrap and serve warm.

Nutritional Facts:

- Calories: 412
- Fats: 22g
- Carbohydrates: 7g
- Proteins: 35g

Salmon With Tzatziki Sauce

Serves: 2

Cook Time: 20 minutes

Ingredients

- FOR THE TZATZIKI SAUCE:
- 140 g Greek-style yogurt
- 1 tablespoon extra virgin olive oil
- 1 tablespoon white wine vinegar
- 1 tablespoon lemon juice
- 1-2 cloves garlic grated or ran through a press
- 1 teaspoon fresh dill or 3/4 teaspoon dried
- kosher salt to taste
- 1 cucumber spiralized or grated
- FOR THE SALMON:
- 2 salmon fillets about 5 ounces each, skins on
- 1 tablespoon extra virgin olive oil
- 1 teaspoon freshly grated lemon zest
- 2 cloves garlic grated or ran through a press (to taste)
- kosher to taste
- freshly ground pepper to taste

Directions

1. FOR THE TZATZIKI SAUCE:
2. In a medium bowl combine yogurt, olive oil, vinegar, lemon juice, garlic, dill and season to taste. If grating the cucumber add it in, if spiralizing it leave it out. Refrigerate covered until needed.
3. FOR THE SALMON:
4. Preheat oven to 400°F/200°C.
5. Mix together in a small bowl olive oil, lemon zest, garlic, and season to taste.
6. Very lightly oil a large piece of foil (about twice the size of your salmon filets). Place salmon skin side down over the foil, and brush with the garlic olive oil. Fold your foil to create an envelope (or in whatever shape you desire, as long as it is sealed closed).
7. Place foil packet on a rimmed baking sheet and bake until just cooked through, 16-20 minutes (cooking times will vary depending on the thickness of your salmon). Be careful when opening the foil envelope, as scalding steam will be released.
8. (Optional), change your oven settings to broil and cook the salmon (tin foil open) for 3-4 minutes to crisp up the top.
9. Remove the salmon from the foil using a spatula. The skins will stick to the foil and your filets will come out in one piece.
10. Serve right away over a bed of cucumber noodles and top it off with the tzatziki sauce.

Nutritional Facts:

- Calories: 440
- Fats: 26g
- Carbohydrates: 5g
- Proteins: 40g

Salmon Stuffed Avocado

Serves: 2

Cook Time: 30 minutes

Ingredients

- 2 small-medium or 1 large avocado, seed removed (200 g / 7.1 oz)
- 2 small salmon fillets (220 g / 7.8 oz) - yields 175 g/ 6.2 oz cooked
- 1 small white onion, finely chopped (70 g / 2.5 oz)
- 1/4 cup soured cream or crème fraîche or mayonnaise, try my home-made mayo (58 g / 2 oz)
- 2 tbsp fresh lemon juice (~ 1/2 lemon)
- salt to taste (I used pink Himalayan)
- freshly ground black pepper to taste
- 1 tbsp ghee or coconut oil (you can make your own ghee)
- 1-2 tbsp freshly chopped dill
- lemon wedges for garnish

Directions

1. Preheat the oven to 200 F / 400 F. Place the salmon filets on a baking tray lined with parchment paper. Drizzle with melted ghee or olive oil, season with salt and pepper and 1 tablespoon of fresh lemon juice. Place in the oven and bake for 20-25 minutes.
2. When done, remove from the oven and let it cool down for 5-10 minutes. Using a fork, shred the salmon fillets and discard the skin. Mix with finely chopped onion, soured cream (or creme fraiche or mayonnaise) and freshly chopped dill.
3. Squeeze in more lemon juice and season with salt and pepper to taste. Scoop the middle of the avocado out leaving 1/2 - 1 inch of the avocado flesh. Cut the scooped avocado into small pieces.
4. Place the chopped avocado into the bowl with salmon and mix until well combined.

5. Fill each avocado half with the salmon & avocado mixture, add lemon and enjoy!

Nutritional Facts:

- Calories: 465
- Fats: 34g
- Carbohydrates: 7g
- Proteins: 27g

Salmon Ceviche

Serves: 4

Cook Time: 30 minutes

Ingredients

- 400 g salmon fillet skinned
- 1/4 cucumber finely cubed
- 2 spring onions chopped diagonally so they look pretty
- handful of coriander leaves
- large lettuce leaves to serve in
- handful of sesame seeds toasted
- juice of 1 lime
- 1 tsp finely grated ginger
- 1 tsp rapeseed oil
- 1 tsp sesame oil
- salt and pepper

Directions

1. Your salmon should be half frozen so you can cut it easier. I used completely frozen salmon fillets, which luckily were not too thick, otherwise it would have been very difficult to cube them. Ideally, stick them in the freezer for half an hour before cutting. Your cubes should be 0.5 cm square.
2. Grate the ginger.
3. Place the salmon cubes in a bowl and pour over the lime juice with the grated ginger. Make sure it is coated well. Chill for 1/2 hour before serving so the salmon can "cook" in the lime juice.
4. Roast your sesame seeds in a pan on a low heat, moving them around regularly so they brown, but do not burn
5. Cube your cucumber, slice your spring onions. After the salmon has been in the fridge for 1/2 hour, add the cucumber, onions, coriander and oil, season with salt and pepper and mix gently.

Nutritional Facts:

- Calories: 200
- Fats: 12g
- Carbohydrates: 2g
- Proteins: 20g

Roasted Salmon With Parmesan Dill Crust

Serves: 2

Cook Time: 10 minutes

Ingredients

- 2 pieces of salmon (about 1.5lbs total)
- ¼ cup mayonnaise

- ¼ cup grated parmesan cheese
- 1 tbsp dill weed
- 1 tsp ground mustard

Directions

1. Preheat oven to 450 degrees.
2. Mix together mayonnaise, parmesan cheese, dill and mustard.
3. Place salmon on a foil-lined baking sheet.
4. Smear half of the mayonnaise mix on top of each piece of salmon.
5. Roast in the oven for about 10 minutes, until the crust is brown and the fish flakes easily.

Nutritional Facts:

- Calories: 660
- Fats: 37g
- Carbohydrates: 10g
- Proteins: 76g

Lemon Butter Baked Cod

Serves: 2

Cook Time: 25 minutes

Ingredients

- 12 ounces cod (fresh or thawed from frozen, less than 1 inch thick and cut into about 4 equal fillets; I use wild Alaskan cod)
- 1/3 cup finely grated parmesan cheese (sandy or powdery texture)
- 1 tablespoon chopped fresh parsley
- 1/2 teaspoon paprika

- 1/4 teaspoon table salt
- For The Sauce:
- 4 cloves garlic, minced
- 1/4 cup dry white wine (I use Sauvignon Blanc)
- 2 tablespoons fresh lemon juice
- 1 tablespoon salted butter

Directions

1. Position an oven rack in the middle of the oven, and preheat to 400 F.
2. Pat the cod fillets dry using paper towels. Sprinkle salt over both sides of each fillet. Set aside while you work on the next steps.
3. In an oven-safe pan large enough to hold all fillets side-by-side (I use a 10-inch nonstick pan), add butter over medium heat. Stir it around until melted, less than 1 minute. Add minced garlic, stirring until aromatic and starting to brown, 1 to 2 minutes.
4. Add white wine and lemon juice to the pan. They should immediately start to simmer. Briefly stir them together and then turn off the heat.
5. In a mixing bowl, stir parmesan cheese with paprika until well-mixed. Place cod fillets side-by-side in the pan, over the sauce. Generously spoon the parmesan mix over the top of the cod fillets in the pan, using a spoon to spread it out until evenly distributed over the fillets. It's fine if some of the parmesan mix falls off the fillets because it'll become part of the sauce.
6. Once the oven has heated to 400 F, transfer the pan to the oven. Bake until the cod fillets are cooked through, 15 to 20 minutes. They are done when they can easily be flaked using a fork. If your fillets are thicker (more than 1 inch in the thickest section), then you may need to bake for an extra 5-10 minutes.
7. Carefully transfer only the cod fillets to serving plates, using a turner spatula to avoid disrupting the parmesan topping, and leaving the liquid in the pan.

8. Stir together the remaining liquid in the pan, optionally boiling over medium-high heat for a minute to thicken the sauce, and drizzle the sauce over the cod. Sprinkle parsley over the cod, and serve while hot.

Nutritional Facts:

- Calories: 280
- Fats: 9g
- Carbohydrates: 3g
- Proteins: 36g

Parmesan Crusted Cod

Serves: 4

Cook Time: 15 minutes

Ingredients

- ¾ cup freshly grated Parmesan cheese
- 2 teaspoons paprika
- 1 tablespoon chopped fresh parsley
- ¼ teaspoon sea salt
- 1 tablespoon extra virgin olive oil
- 4 cod fillets (about 6 oz. each)
- lemon wedges (optional: for serving) cut into wedges

Directions

1. Preheat the oven to 400°F. Line a baking sheet with parchment paper or foil.

2. In a shallow bowl, mix together the Parmesan, paprika, parsley and salt. Drizzle the cod with olive oil (rubbing it into the front and back of the fillet), then dredge in the cheese mixture, pressing it in lightly with your fingers. Transfer to the baking sheet. Top cod with any leftover cheese mixture.
3. Bake until the fish is opaque in the thickest part, 10-15 minutes. Serve with the lemon slices.

Nutritional Facts:

- Calories: 115
- Fats: 6g
- Carbohydrates: 2g
- Proteins: 10g

Buttered Cod Skillet

Serves: 4

Cook Time: 5 minutes

Ingredients

- Cod-
- 1 1/2 lbs cod fillets
- 6 Tbsp unsalted butter, sliced
- Seasoning-
- ¼ tsp garlic powder
- ½ tsp table salt
- ¼ tsp ground pepper
- ¾ tsp ground paprika

- Few lemon slices
- Herbs, parsley or cilantro

Directions

1. Stir together ingredients for seasoning in a small bowl.
2. Cut cod into smaller pieces, if desired. Season all sides of the cod with the seasoning.
3. Heat 2 Tbsp butter in a large skillet over medium-high heat. Once butter melts, add cod to skillet. Cook 2 minutes.
4. Turn heat down to medium. Turn cod over, top with remaining butter and cook another 3-4 minutes.
5. Butter will completely melt and the fish will cook. (Don't overcook the cod, it will become mushy and completely fall apart.)
6. Drizzle cod with fresh lemon juice. Top with fresh herbs, if desired. Serve immediately.
7. Enjoy, friends.

Nutritional Facts:

- Calories: 494
- Fats: 18g
- Carbohydrates: 2g
- Proteins: 30g

Shrimp & Bacon Zoodle Alfredo

Serves: 2

Cook Time: 20 minutes

Ingredients

- 1/4 cup butter
- 2 Tbsp garlic
- 1 lbs shrimp, peeled and deveined
- 1/2 teaspoon sea salt
- 1/2 teaspoon fresh cracked pepper
- 1 teaspoon paprika
- 4 cooked bacon strips, chopped (optional)
- 3 medium zucchini, julienned or spiralized
- 1/3 cup heavy cream
- 1/4 cup parmesan cheese

Directions

1. In a skillet, melt butter over medium-high heat. Once bubbling, toss in garlic and and shrimp. Sprinkle with salt, pepper and paprika. Cook on both sides until cooked through. Transfer to a bowl with a slotted spoon.
2. Toss zucchini into pan, drizzle with cream. Cook just until warm. Remove from heat. Sprinkle with parmesan. Serve topped with shrimp. Enjoy!

Nutritional Facts:

- Calories: 494
- Fats: 40g
- Carbohydrates: 2g
- Proteins: 53g

8. CHICKEN

Chicken Cacciatore
Serves: 2

Cook Time: 35 minutes

Ingredients

- 4 chicken thighs, with the bone, skin removed
- kosher salt and fresh pepper to taste
- olive oil spray
- 1/2 can, 14 oz crushed tomatoes (Tuttorosso my favorite!)
- 1/2 cup diced onion
- 1/4 cup diced red bell pepper
- 1/2 cup diced green bell pepper
- 1/2 teaspoon dried oregano
- 1 bay leaf
- 2 tablespoons chopped basil or parsley for topping

Directions

1. Season chicken with salt and pepper on both side.
2. Press saute on the Instant Pot, lightly spray with oil and brown chicken on both sides a few minutes. Set aside.
3. Spray with a little more oil and add onions and peppers. Sauté until soften and golden, 5 minutes.
4. Pour tomatoes over the chicken and vegetables, add oregano, bay leaf, salt and pepper, give it a quick stir and cover.
5. Cook high pressure 25 minutes; natural release.
6. Remove bay leaf, garnish with parsley and serve over pasta, squasta or whatever you wish!

Nutritional Facts:

- Calories: 133
- Fats: 10g
- Carbohydrates: 10g
- Proteins: 14g

One-Pot Bacon Garlic Chicken and Spinach Dinner

Serves: 2

Cook Time: 15 minutes

Ingredients

- 3 slices bacon
- 3-5 lbs Chicken, skinless, chicken thighs - unrolled to lay flat
- 2 tbsp chicken stock, + 1/2 cup low sodium
- 1 tbsp butter
- 2 tbsp garlic, diced
- 1 1/2 cup spinach, fresh

Directions

1. In a large, heavy pan, cook and crisp bacon until well browned.
2. Remove bacon from pan, do not drain grease, and set aside and crumble when cool (while chicken is cooking).
3. Add chicken thighs to pan (I like to lay them flat to crisp up more and let the fat render).
4. Let brown on each side, about 4-6 minutes.
5. Remove from pan when browned and set aside (chicken may not be fully cooked, we're just trying to get it well browned at this point.)

6. Add 2 tbsp stock to pan, scrape any bits of chicken that stuck to pan with stock with a rubber spatula (don't scrub with metal on a cast iron pan, if using something else metal is ok)
7. Add butter to pan, let melt.
8. Add garlic to pan, let brown, about 4 minutes. Make sure garlic does not burn.
9. Add stock to pan, and then add chicken thighs back in.
10. Cook until stock has reduced into a thicker sauce and chicken has reached internal temperature of 165 degrees - about 5 minutes.
11. Add spinach, toss with chicken and sauce, and let reduce.
12. Sprinkle crumbled bacon over the top.
13. When spinach is soft and reduced, remove from heat and serve!

Nutritional Facts:

- Calories: 465
- Fats: 10g
- Carbohydrates: 2g
- Proteins: 31g

Lemon and Herb Roast Chicken

Serves: 4

Cook Time: 60 minutes

Ingredients

- 1 whole chicken (approximately 4½ pounds)
- 4 tablespoons unsalted butter, at room temperature
- 3 lemons, halved
- ½ bunch thyme
- ½ bunch rosemary

- Salt and freshly ground black pepper

Directions

1. Preheat the oven to 425°F. Line a baking sheet with aluminum foil and place a roasting rack on top.
2. Rinse the chicken and pat dry very well with paper towels. Bend the wings back around the neck of the chicken.
3. Rub the chicken all around the outside with the softened butter. Stuff the inside of the chicken with the lemon halves and the herbs. Season the chicken inside and out with salt and pepper.
4. Tie the legs of the chicken together with trussing twine and cut away excess strings.
5. Transfer the chicken to the prepared roasting rack. Roast until the skin is golden brown, 35 to 40 minutes. Reduce the heat to 375°F and continue roasting until the chicken is cooked through (the juice between the leg and thigh runs clear, and a meat thermometer reads 165°F).
6. Let the chicken rest for 15 to 20 minutes before carving and serving.

Nutritional Facts:

- Calories: 616
- Fats: 45g
- Carbohydrates: 5g
- Proteins: 44g

Chicken with 40 Garlic Cloves

Serves: 6

Cook Time: 45 minutes

Ingredients

- 2 lbs chicken thighs boneless and skinless
- 2 tbsp olive oil
- 40 cloves garlic cleaned but kept whole
- 1/2 tsp salt or to taste
- 1/4 tsp pepper or to taste
- 1/2 tsp cumin
- 1 tsp fresh dill
- 1/2 tsp dried thyme
- 1/2 cup white wine
- 1/2 cup chicken broth low sodium
- 1 tbsp fresh parsley chopped for garnish

Directions

1. Preheat oven: Preheat oven to 375 F degrees.
2. Prepare chicken: Clean the chicken thighs, pat them dry and cut them in half.
3. Cook chicken: In a large Dutch oven or oven proof skillet add the olive oil and heat over medium-high heat. Add chicken thighs and cook on both sides just until they start to brown and are no longer pink. Transfer the chicken to a plate.
4. Cook garlic: Add the cloves of garlic to the same skillet. Season with cumin, dill, thyme, salt, pepper and stir. Add the wine, stir a bit and scrape all the pieces from the bottom of the skillet, then cook for about 2 minutes just until the wine reduces a bit and the garlic starts to brown.

5. Finish cooking: Stir in the chicken broth then add the chicken back to the skillet. Cover the skillet with a lid and place in the oven for about 20 minutes.
6. Garnish and serve: Garnish with parsley and serve warm over rice or noodles.

Nutritional Facts:

- Calories: 420
- Fats: 29g
- Carbohydrates: 7g
- Proteins: 25g

Creamy Sun Dried Tomato and Parmesan Chicken Zoodles
Serves: 6

Cook Time: 15 minutes

Ingredients

- 1 tablespoon butter
- 700 g | 1 1/2 lb skinless chicken thigh fillets, cut into strips
- 120 g | 4oz fresh semi-dried tomato strips in oil, chopped *See Notes
- 100 g | 3.5oz jarred sun dried tomatoes in oil, chopped
- 4 cloves garlic, peeled and crushed
- 300 ml | 1 1/4 cup thickened cream, reduced fat or full fat (or half and half)
- 1 cup shaved Parmesan cheese
- Salt to taste
- Dried basil seasoning
- Red chilli flakes

- 2 large Zucchini (or summer squash), made into Zoodles (use a vegetable grater if you don't have a Zoodle grater)

Directions

1. Heat the butter in a pan/skillet over medium high heat. Add the chicken strips and sprinkle with salt. Pan fry until the chicken is golden browned on all sides and cooked through.
2. Add both semi-dried and sun dried tomatoes with 1 tablespoon of the oil from the jar (optional but adds extra flavour), and add the garlic; sauté until fragrant. (While the chicken is browning, prepare your Zoodles with a Zoodle maker OR with a normal vegetable peeler.)
3. Lower heat, add the cream and the Parmesan cheese; simmer while stirring until the cheese has melted through. Sprinkle over salt, basil and red chilli flakes to your taste.
4. Stir through the Zoodles and continue to simmer until the zoodles have softened to your liking (about 5-8 minutes) and serve.

Nutritional Facts:

- Calories: 395
- Fats: 22g
- Carbohydrates: 9g
- Proteins: 35g

Sheet Pan Chicken Fajitas

Serves: 6

Cook Time: 30 minutes

Ingredients

- 1 1/2 pounds of chicken breast tenders
- 1 yellow bell pepper sliced into 1/4 inch slices
- 1 red bell pepper sliced into 1/4 inch slices
- 1 orange bell pepper sliced into 1/4 inch slices
- 1 small red onion sliced into 1/4 inch slices
- 1 1/2 tablespoons of extra virgin olive oil
- 1 teaspoon of kosher salt
- several turns of freshly ground pepper
- 2 teaspoon of chili powder
- 1/2 teaspoon of garlic powder
- 1/2 teaspoon of onion powder
- 1/2 teaspoon of ground cumin
- 1/2 teaspoon of smoked paprika
- lime
- fresh cilantro for garnish
- tortillas warmed

Directions

1. Preheat oven to 425 degrees.
2. In a large bowl, combine onion, bell pepper, chicken tenders, olive oil, salt and pepper and spices.
3. Toss to combine.
4. Spray baking sheet with non stick cooking spray.
5. Spread chicken, bell peppers and onions on baking sheet.
6. Cook at 425 degrees for about 20 minutes, until chicken reaches 165 degrees. Then turn oven to broil and cook for additional 1-2

minutes just letting the veggies pick up some color. Watch carefully to make sure they don't start to burn.
7. In the last five minutes of cooking, not while the broiler is on, let tortillas wrapped in foil warm in the oven.
8. Squeeze juice from fresh limes over fajita mixture while hot and top with fresh cilantro.
9. Serve in warm tortillas.

Nutritional Facts:

- Calories: 395
- Fats: 22g
- Carbohydrates: 9g
- Proteins: 35g

Italian Chicken Meal Prep

Serves: 4

Cook Time: 20 minutes

Ingredients

- 1 tsp salt
- 1/2 tsp pepper
- 2 tsp basil
- 2 tsp marjoram
- 2 tsp rosemary
- 2 tsp thyme
- 1 tsp. paprika
- 2 lbs boneless skinless chicken breasts cut into bite sized pieces
- 1 1/2 cup broccoli florets
- 1 small red onion chopped

- 1 cup plum tomatoes
- 1 medium zucchini chopped
- 2 tsp garlic minced
- 2 Tbs olive oil
- 2-4 cups cooked rice of choice optional

Directions

1. Pre-heat oven to 450F. Line a baking sheet with aluminum foil and set aside.
2. In a small bowl, mix salt, pepper, basil, marjoram, rosemary, thyme, and paprika
3. Place the chicken and veggies in the baking dish. Sprinkle all the spices and garlic evenly over the chicken and veggies. Drizzle with the olive oil.
4. Bake for 15-20 minutes until chicken is cooked, and veggies are slightly charred.
5. Broil 1-2 minutes to brown chicken
6. Place ½ or 1 cup of cooked rice of choice into 4 individual meal prep containers.
7. Divide chicken and veggies evenly on top of the rice.
8. Cover and store in the fridge for 3- 5 days or serve for dinner!

Nutritional Facts:

- Calories: 305
- Fats: 7g
- Carbohydrates: 7g
- Proteins: 53g

Chicken, Avocado and Goat Cheese Salad

Serves: 4

Cook Time: 10 minutes

Ingredients

- 1 pound boneless skinless chicken tenders
- 1/4 cup extra virgin olive oil
- 4 cloves garlic, minced or grated
- 1/4 cup fresh parsley, chopped (or 1 tablespoon dried)
- 1/4 cup fresh basil, chopped (or 1 tablespoon dried)
- 1/2 teaspoon smoked paprika
- 1/2 teaspoon onion powder
- 1/4 teaspoon cayenne
- 1/2 teaspoon kosher salt and pepper
- 2 heads romaine lettuce, chopped
- 1 cup fresh strawberries, halved
- 2 watermelon radishes, thinly slice
- 2 Persian cucumbers, sliced
- 4 ounces herbed goat cheese, crumbled
- 1 avocado, sliced
- 1/2 cup roasted almonds, chopped
- large handful micro greens, sprouts, and or edible flowers, for serving
- HONEY BALSAMIC VINAIGRETTE
- 1/4 cup olive oil
- 1/4 cup balsamic vinegar
- 2 tablespoons apple cider vinegar
- 1 tablespoon honey
- pinch of cayenne (to taste)
- kosher salt and pepper

Directions

1. In a bowl, combine the chicken, olive oil, garlic, parsley, basil, paprika, onion powder, cayenne, salt, and pepper. For added flavor, allow the chicken to marinate 1 hour or overnight.
2. Preheat your grill, grill pan or cast iron skillet to medium high and brush the grates with oil.
3. Grill the chicken for 5-8 minutes per side or until the chicken is cooked through. Remove from the grill and thinly slice the chicken.
4. In a large salad bowl, toss together the lettuce, strawberries, radishes, and cucumbers. Add the chicken on top of the salad along with the goat cheese, avocado, almonds, and a handful of micro greens. Serve with the honey balsamic (below).
5. HONEY BALSAMIC VINAIGRETTE
6. In a glass jar, combine the olive oil, balsamic vinegar, apple cider vinegar, honey, cayenne, and a pinch each of salt and pepper. Seal the jar and shake well. Taste and adjust seasonings as needed. Keep stored in the fridge for up to 1 week.

Nutritional Facts:

- Calories: 305
- Fats: 7g
- Carbohydrates: 7g
- Proteins: 53g

Creamy Pesto Parmesan Chicken

Serves: 4

Cook Time: 25 minutes

Ingredients

- 4 boneless skinless chicken breasts, pounded to even thickness OR 4-6 chicken thighs
- 1/2 cup sliced mushrooms
- 1 teaspoon minced garlic
- 1/3 cup basil pesto
- 1/3 cup chicken broth
- 1/3 cup heavy cream
- 1/4 cup shaved or grated parmesan cheese, plus more for topping
- salt and pepper to taste
- fresh basil, for topping (optional)

Directions

1. Grease a large skillet and cook chicken over medium heat 5-8 minutes on each side until browned on the outside and cooked through. Transfer to a plate and cover to keep warm.
2. Add garlic and mushrooms to pan and saute over medium heat til garlic fragrant and mushrooms are tender, about 3-4 minutes.
3. Add pesto to pan and saute 1-2 minutes. Add chicken broth and stir to combine with pesto. Add cream and continue to stir over medium heat until sauce is smooth. Add parmesan cheese and stir until melted and combined with sauce. Taste and add salt and pepper if needed, to taste.
4. Return chicken to pan and toss in the sauce to coat. Sprinkle additional parmesan cheese over the chicken and garnish with fresh basil and serve.

Nutritional Facts:

- Calories: 351
- Fats: 21g
- Carbohydrates: 7g
- Proteins: 20g

One Pan Pizza Chicken

Serves: 4

Cook Time: 25 minutes

Ingredients

- 4 boneless, skinless chicken breasts
- Kosher salt and freshly ground black pepper, to taste
- 2 tablespoons olive oil
- 3 cloves garlic, minced
- 1 (28-ounce) can crushed tomatoes
- 1 teaspoon dried basil
- 1/2 teaspoon dried oregano
- 1/2 teaspoon dried parsley
- 1/2 teaspoon crushed red pepper flakes, optional
- 1 cup shredded mozzarella cheese
- 1/4 cup mini pepperoni
- 1/4 cup basil leaves

Directions

1. Preheat oven to broil.
2. Season chicken with salt and pepper, to taste.

3. Heat olive oil in a large skillet over medium heat. Add chicken and cook, flipping once, until cooked through, about 4-5 minutes on each side; set aside.
4. Add garlic to the skillet, and cook, stirring frequently, until fragrant, about 1-2 minutes.
5. Stir in crushed tomatoes, basil, oregano, parsley and red pepper flakes; season with salt and pepper, to taste.
6. Bring to a boil; reduce heat to low and simmer, stirring occasionally, until sauce has thickened, about 15-20 minutes.
7. Return chicken to the skillet. Top with mozzarella and mini pepperonis.
8. Place into oven and cook until melted and golden brown, about 2 minutes.
9. Serve immediately, garnished with basil, if desired.

Nutritional Facts:

- Calories: 351
- Fats: 21g
- Carbohydrates: 7g
- Proteins: 20g

Chicken with Poblano Peppers and Cream

Serves: 4

Cook Time: 25 minutes

Ingredients

- 1 1/4 pounds boneless-skinless chicken filets
- 2 medium roasted poblano peppers cut into strips
- 3 1/2 ounces medium onion sliced 1/4-inch thick

- 1 large clove garlic, sliced
- 1/4 cup dry white wine
- 1 cup heavy cream
- 1/8 teaspoon dried cumin
- 1 tablespoon olive oil, divided
- salt and pepper to taste

Directions

1. Peppers: Roast the poblano peppers until all sides are blackened. If you have a gas stove, place them right on the burner over medium-low heat, turning and re-positioning until the are blistered and black on all sides. If not, place directly under a broiler or on a grill. Put into a bowl and cover with plastic wrap so they can steam for 5-10 minutes before peeling. Cut and proceed with the recipe or refrigerate until needed.
2. Chicken: Let the chicken come to temperature on the counter for about 20 minutes. Place a stainless steal or non-stick skillet and 2 teaspoons of the oil over medium high heat (NOT A CAST IRON SKILLET.) Blot the chicken dry, massage with the remaining teaspoon of oil and season with salt and pepper. When pan is hot, cook the chicken 4-6 minutes per side or until an instant read thermometer registers 160. Remove the chicken to a plate and tent with foil.
3. Sauce: Turn the heat down to medium and saute the onions and garlic for about 1 minute. Remove the pan from the heat and add the wine. Place the pan back over the heat and cook until most of the wine has evaporated, scraping up any browned bits left from the chicken. Add the cream, poblano peppers and cumin. Cook until the cream has thickened to your liking keeping in mind that it will become even thicker as it cools. Taste the sauce and adjust salt and pepper as necessary. Serve over the chicken.
4. Variation: If you'd like, add the cooked onion and garlic, poblano peppers and cream to a blender and blend until smooth. Return to

the pan, add the cumin and cook until thickened. If it becomes too thick, add a little chicken broth. Salt and pepper to taste.

Nutritional Facts:

- Calories: 484
- Fats: 40g
- Carbohydrates: 6g
- Proteins: 20g

Caprese Hasselback Chicken

Serves: 4

Cook Time: 25 minutes

Ingredients

- 4 large chicken breasts, (6 ounces each)
- 4 oz fresh mozzarella cheese, the kind that comes in a log
- 2 medium roma tomatoes, sliced
- 1/4 cup fresh basil, divided (half of it cut into ribbons)
- 2 tbsp olive oil
- 2 tbsp balsamic vinegar
- sea salt & pepper

Directions

1. Preheat the oven to 400 degrees F. Line a baking sheet with parchment paper or foil.
2. Make 5-6 deep slits in each chicken breast, being careful not to cut all the way through. Season both sides with sea salt and black pepper. Place onto the lined baking sheet.

3. Slice the tomatoes and mozzarella very thinly, about 1/8" to 1/4" thick, and cut the pieces to a width slightly wider than the thickness of your chicken breast. Stuff a piece of mozzarella, a tomato slice, and a whole basil leaf into each slit in the chicken.
4. Drizzle olive oil and balsamic vinegar over the chicken.
5. Bake for 20-25 minutes, until cooked through (heated to 160 degrees F with a meat thermometer).
6. When the chicken is ready, sprinkle remaining fresh basil ribbons on top right before serving. If desired, drizzle with additional balsamic vinegar.

Nutritional Facts:

- Calories: 365
- Fats: 21g
- Carbohydrates: 4g
- Proteins: 40g

Shredded Chicken Chili

Serves: 6

Cook Time: 25 minutes

Ingredients

- 4 chicken breasts large, shredded
- 1 tbsp Butter
- ½ onion chopped
- 2 cups Chicken broth
- 10 oz diced tomatoes canned, undrained
- 2 oz tomato paste
- 1 tbsp Chili powder
- 1 tbsp Cumin

- 1/2 tbsp Garlic powder
- 1 jalapeno pepper chopped (optional)
- 4 oz Cream cheese
- Salt and pepper to taste

Directions

1. Prepare chicken by boiling chicken breasts in water or broth on stovetop for 10-12 minutes, just barely covered in liquid. Once the meat is no longer pink, remove from fluid and shred with two forks. This same technique can also be used with a pressure cooker at pressure for 5 minutes with a natural release, or a slow cooker for 4-6 hours. Whatever's clever for you! Rotisserie chicken meat can be substituted for the breasts as well.
2. In a large stockpot, melt the butter over medium-high heat. Add the onion and cook until translucent.
3. Add the shredded chicken, chicken broth, diced tomatoes, tomato paste, chili powder, cumin, garlic powder, and jalapeno to the pot and combine by gently stirring over the burner. Bring to a boil, then drop it down to a simmer over medium-low heat and cover for 10 minutes.
4. Cut cream cheese into small, 1-inch chunks.
5. Remove lid and mix in the cream cheese. Increase the heat back up to medium-high and continue to stir until the cream cheese is completely blended in. Remove from heat and season with salt and pepper to taste.
6. Eat as-is or garnish with toppings of your choice. I love cilantro and Monterey jack cheese for ooey gooey goodness.

Nutritional Facts:

- Calories: 200
- Fats: 11g
- Carbohydrates: 7g
- Proteins: 19g

9. SMOOTHIES

Acai Almond Butter Smoothie
Serves: 1

Prep Time: 5 minutes

Ingredients

- 1 100g Pack Unsweetened Acai Puree
- 3/4 cup Unsweetened Almond Milk
- 1/4 of an Avocado
- 3 tbsp Collagen or Protein Powder
- 1 tbsp Coconut Oil or MCT Oil Powder
- 1 tbsp Almond Butter
- 1/2 tsp Vanilla Extract
- 2 drops Liquid Stevia (optional)

Directions

1. If you are using individualized 100 gram packs of acai puree, run the pack under lukewarm water for a few seconds until you are able to break up the puree into smaller pieces. Open the pack and put the contents into the blender.
2. Place the remaining ingredients in the blender and blend until smooth. Add more water or ice cubes as needed.
3. Drizzle the almond butter along the side of the glass to make it look cool.
4. Enjoy and pat yourself on the back for an awesome workout and killer post workout smoothie!

Nutritional Facts:

- Calories: 345
- Fats: 20g
- Carbohydrates: 8g
- Proteins: 15g

Blueberry Galaxy Smoothie

Serves: 1

Prep Time: 5 minutes

Ingredients

- 1 cup Coconut Milk or almond milk
- 1/4 cup Blueberries
- 1 tsp Vanilla Extract
- 1 tsp MCT Oil or coconut oil
- 30 g Protein Powder optional

Directions

1. Put all the ingredients into a blender, and blend until smooth.

Nutritional Facts:

- Calories: 343
- Fats: 21g
- Carbohydrates: 3g
- Proteins: 31g
-

Clean and Green Smoothie

Serves: 1

Prep Time: 5 minutes

Ingredients

- 1 cup filtered water
- 1/2 avocado
- 1 tablespoon MCT oil
- 1/2 organic cucumber
- 1 large handful dark leafy greens
- 1 – 2 leaves dandelion
- 2 tablespoons parsley
- 2 tablespoons hemp seeds
- Juice from 1 lemon
- ¼ teaspoon turmeric powder

Directions

1. Blend all ingredients in a high-speed blender until smooth, about 1 minute. Best enjoyed cold.

Nutritional Facts:

- Calories: 360
- Fats: 22g
- Carbohydrates: 12g
- Proteins: 10g

Frozen Berry Shake

Serves: 1

Prep Time: 5 minutes

Ingredients

- 1/3 cup creamed coconut milk or heavy whipping cream (80 ml/ 2.7 fl oz)
- 1/2 cup water or unsweetened almond milk (120 ml/ 4 fl oz)
- 1/2 cup mixed frozen berries (75 g/ 2.6 oz)
- 1 tbsp MCT oil or virgin coconut oil
- few ice cubes, to taste
- Optionally add:
- 3-5 drops Stevia extract
- 1/2 tsp sugar-free vanilla extract
- whipped cream or coconut milk on top

Directions

1. To "cream" the coconut milk, simply place the can in the fridge overnight. Next day, open, spoon out the solidified coconut milk and discard the liquids. Do not shake before opening the can. One 400 gram can will yield about 200 grams of coconut cream.
2. Place the creamed coconut milk, berries, water or almond milk and ice into a blender.
3. Add MCT oil and stevia (optional).
4. Pulse until smooth and serve immediately. Optionally, top with whipped cream or coconut milk.

Nutritional Facts:

- Calories: 400
- Fats: 40g

- Carbohydrates: 10g
- Proteins: 4g

Green Low-Carb Breakfast Smoothie

Serves: 1

Prep Time: 5 minutes

Ingredients

- 1.5 cups almond milk
- 1 oz spinach
- 50 grams cucumber
- 50 grams celery
- 50 grams avocado
- 1 tbsp coconut oil
- 10 drops liquid stevia
- 1 scoop Isopure Protein Powder (about 30 grams)
- 1/2 tsp chia seeds (to garnish)
- 1 tsp matcha powder (optional)

Directions

1. Into a blender or Nutribullet, add your almond milk and spinach. Blend for a second to break down the spinach to make room for the rest of the ingredients.
2. Add in the rest of your ingredients and blend for about a minute until creamy.
3. You can add a teaspoon of matcha powder for added benefits and a kick of caffeine.
4. Pour it into a glass and garnish with chia seeds. Enjoy!

Nutritional Facts:

- Calories: 375
- Fats: 25g
- Carbohydrates: 4g
- Proteins: 30g

Minty Green Protein Smoothie

Serves: 1

Prep Time: 5 minutes

Ingredients

- 1/2 avocado
- 1 cup fresh spinach
- 10-12 drops Liquid Stevia Peppermint Sweet Drops
- 1 scoop whey protein powder
- 1/2 cup unsweetened almond milk
- 1/4 tsp peppermint extract
- 1 cup ice

Directions

1. Place avocado, spinach, protein powder and milk in a blender and blend until smooth. Add the Liquid Stevia Peppermint Sweet Drops, extract, and ice, and blend until thick. Taste and adjust stevia, as needed.

Nutritional Facts:

- Calories: 282

- Fats: 20g
- Carbohydrates: 14g
- Proteins: 14g

Blueberry Coconut Chia Smoothie

Serves: 1

Prep Time: 5 minutes

Ingredients

- 1 cup frozen blueberries
- 1 cup full fat Greek yogurt (you can use almond milk or coconut milk yogurt for dairy-free and vegan options)
- 1/2 cup coconut cream (the really thick creamy stuff from the top of the can of full fat coconut milk)
- 1 cup unsweetened cashew or almond milk
- 2 tbsp coconut oil
- 2 tbsp ground chia seed
- 2 Tbsp Swerve Sweetener or equivalent sweetener (use your favourite!)
- Feel free to add protein powder, collagen or any other supplement that appeals to you.

Directions

1. Combine all ingredients in blender and blend until smooth.
2. Divide among 4 glasses and serve.

Nutritional Facts:

- Calories: 450
- Fats: 20g
- Carbohydrates: 11g
- Proteins: 7g

Cinnamon Almond Butter Breakfast Shake

Serves: 1

Prep Time: 5 minutes

Ingredients

- 1 1/2 cups unsweetened nut milk
- 1 scoop collagen peptides
- 2 Tbsp almond butter
- 2 Tbsp golden flax meal
- ½ tsp cinnamon
- 15 drops liquid stevia
- 1/8 tsp almond extract
- 1/8 tsp salt
- 6–8 ice cubes

Directions

1. Add all the ingredients to a blender and combine for 30 seconds or until you get a smooth consistency.

Nutritional Facts:

- Calories: 326
- Fats: 27g

- Carbohydrates: 11g
- Proteins: 19g

Chocolate Coconut Keto Smoothie Bowl

Serves: 1

Prep Time: 5 minutes

Ingredients

- 3/4 cup full-fat canned organic coconut milk (BPA-free)
- 2 tablespoons unsweetened raw cacao powder or unsweetened cocoa powder
- 15-20 drops liquid coconut stevia (or plain stevia to taste)
- Handful of ice (just enough to thicken)
- 2 scoops collagen protein

Directions

1. Place all of the ingredients except the collagen in a blender and blend well.
2. Add the collagen and gently pulse until blended to avoid damaging delicate proteins.
3. Place in a bowl and add optional garnishes. Enjoy immediately, or chill in the freezer for 30 minutes for a thicker consistency.

Nutritional Facts:

- Calories: 500
- Fats: 38g
- Carbohydrates: 12g
- Proteins: 22g

Chocolate Mint Avocado Smoothie

Serves: 1

Prep Time: 5 minutes

Ingredients

- 1/2 cup coconut milk
- 1 cup water
- 1/2 cup ice
- 2 scoops of Chocolate Collagen Protein
- 1/2 a frozen avocado
- 4 mint leaves
- 1 tablespoon of crushed cacao butter
- 2 tablespoons of shredded coconut

Directions

1. Add all ingredients excluding the collagen protein and shredded coconut to a blender.
2. Blend for 45 seconds on high.
3. Add collagen protein and blend for 5 seconds on low
4. Top with coconut flakes.

Nutritional Facts:

- Calories: 552
- Fats: 44g
- Carbohydrates: 10g
- Proteins: 26g

Keto Green Smoothie

Serves: 2

Prep Time: 5 minutes

Ingredients

- 1 cup cold water
- 1 cup baby spinach
- 1/2 cup cilantro
- 1 inch ginger peeled
- 3/4 English cucumber peeled
- 1/2-1 lemon peeled
- 1 cup frozen avocado

Directions

1. Add all ingredients to a high speed blender and blend until smooth.
2. Store in an air-tight container such as a mason jar in the fridge for up to 3 days.

Nutritional Facts:

- Calories: 148
- Fats: 11g
- Carbohydrates: 13g
- Proteins: 2g

Cucumber Green Tea Detox Smoothie

Serves: 2

Prep Time: 5 minutes

Ingredients

- 8 ounces water
- 2 tsp Match Green Tea powder
- 1 cup sliced cucumber
- 2 ounces ripe avocado
- 1 tsp lemon juice
- 1/2 tsp lemon liquid stevia
- 1/2 cup ice

Directions

1. Pour the water and green tea powder into a bender first and give it a whir to combine.
2. Add the remaining ingredients and blend on high until smooth.
3. Taste and adjust sweetener as desired.
4. Enjoy immediately or refrigerate until ready to serve.

Nutritional Facts:

- Calories: 69
- Fats: 4g
- Carbohydrates: 6g
- Proteins: 2g

No-Sugar Kale & Coconut Shake

Serves: 1

Prep Time: 5 minutes

Ingredients

- 1 cup unsweetened almond milk (substitute your favorite non-dairy milk)
- 1/2 cup full-fat canned coconut milk
- 4 cups chopped kale (you can also do a mix of spinach & kale)
- 1/4 cup ground coconut (unsweetened)
- 1 1-inch piece fresh ginger, peeled (optional--skip it if you don't like the taste of ginger)
- 1/4 teaspoon kosher salt (or Celtic sea salt if you have it--it's rich in beneficial minerals!)
- 1 cup ice

Directions

1. Pour almond and coconut milk into base of blender, followed by ginger, kale, ground coconut, salt, and ice.
2. Puree until very smooth.

Nutritional Facts:

- Calories: 269
- Fats: 24g
- Carbohydrates: 10g
- Proteins: 12g
-

Chai Pumpkin Keto Smoothie

Serves: 1

Prep Time: 5 minutes

Ingredients

- 3/4 cup full-fat coconut milk
- 3 tablespoons pumpkin puree
- 1 tablespoon MCT oil, optional
- 1 teaspoon loose chai tea
- 1 teaspoon alcohol-free vanilla
- ½ teaspoon pumpkin pie spice
- ½ fresh or frozen avocado

Directions

1. Add all ingredients but avocado to the blender and blend until smooth. Add the avocado and blend until broken apart.
2. Serve with a sprinkle of pumpkin spice on top, if you'd like.

Nutritional Facts:

- Calories: 276
- Fats: 70g
- Carbohydrates: 19g
- Proteins: 5g

Raspberry Avocado Smoothie
Serves: 1

Prep Time: 5 minutes

Ingredients

- 1 ripe avocado peeled and pit removed
- 1 1/3 cup water
- 2-3 tablespoons lemon juice
- 2 Tbsp low carb sweetener I like to use 1/8 teaspoon liquid stevia extract
- 1/2 cup frozen unsweetened raspberries or other low carb frozen berries

Directions

1. Add all ingredients to blender.
2. Blend until smooth.
3. Pour into two tall glasses and enjoy with a straw!

Nutritional Facts:

- Calories: 227
- Fats: 20g
- Carbohydrates: 12g
- Proteins: 3g

Conclusion

I hope you enjoyed our cookbook.

A ketogenic diet plan benefits your health through a metabolic switch in the primary cellular fuel source to which your body and brain are adapted. When your metabolism switches from relying on carbohydrate-based fuels (glucose from starch and sugar) to fat-based fuels and fat metabolism products called ketones, positive changes at a cellular level occur, and this translates into better overall health.

Being in nutritional ketosis is a beneficial body state, and a great deal of research is being done on ketosis as it relates to disease. Ketone bodies themselves are useful and have been shown to alleviate many disease conditions through the improvement of cellular energy pathways and mitochondrial health.

Ketogenic diets are now being used to treat medical conditions such as diabetes, epilepsy, autism, Alzheimer's, cancer, and others and much of the success of these treatments is rooted in these cellular effects.

Made in the
USA
Lexington, KY